PAST and PRESENT

No 13

BRITISH RAILWAYS PAST & PRESENT No 13: NORTH WEST, WEST AND SOUTH WEST LONDON - This book presents a detailed examination of the changing face of the railways in the region depicted in this map, which includes locations featured in the photographs or mentioned in the text. The pictures have been chosen to provide a balanced view, including railways which are still in use or being developed, together with scenes where the lines have been closed and either abandoned or redeveloped since the 'past' pictures were taken.

BRITISH RAILWAYS

PAST and PRESENT

No 13
North West, West and South West London

Brian Morrison & Ken Brunt

SLP

Silver Link Publishing Ltd

First published in July 1992

British Library Cataloguing in Publication Data

A catalogue record for this book is available from the British Library.

ISBN 0 947971 80 7

Silver Link Publishing Ltd
The Trundle
Ringstead Road
Great Addington
Kettering
Northants NN14 4BW

Maps drawn by Christina Siviter

Printed in Great Britain by
Woolnough Bookbinding Ltd, Irthlingborough, Northants,
and bound by Butler & Tanner Ltd, Frome, Somerset

WESTERN JUNCTION, DALSTON: On 15 October 1984, the 10.37 Broad Street-Richmond train is formed of a Class '501' electric multiple unit (EMU) No 501157, while a Gloucester RC&W Class '119' cross-country diesel multiple unit (DMU) in the platform at Dalston Kingsland station awaits its passing before proceeding to Old Oak Common as empty coaching stock (ECS) following works attention at Stratford.

By 30 April 1991 the line from Broad Street has disappeared and the North London Line is electrified and runs through from North Woolwich to Richmond without the change previously necessary at Gospel Oak. Restarting from the Dalston Kingsland stop, Class '313' EMU No 313010 forms the 11.35 train from North Woolwich to Richmond. Very little has happened to the background buildings, and Western Junction signal box structure still exists together with Dalston Kingsland station, just visible beneath the road bridge. *Both Brian Morrison*

CONTENTS

Introduction   7

Paddington   9
Old Oak Common (81A)   15
Westward from Paddington   19
West London Line   29

Waterloo   36
Nine Elms (70A)   45
South Western Lines   49
Feltham (70B)   69

North London Line   71

Marylebone   76
Neasden (34E)   80
Chiltern Lines   81

Victoria   91
Stewarts Lane (73A)   94
South London Line   96
Surrey suburbs   99

Euston   105
Camden Bank   108
Camden (1B)   111
Willesden (1A)   117
Into Middlesex and Herts   118

St Pancras   129
Kentish Town (14B)   132
Cricklewood (14A)   134
The Midland Main Line   136

Index of locations   144

BIBLIOGRAPHY

A Regional History of the Railways of Great Britain, Vol 3 Greater London *by H. P. White (David & Charles)*

London's Local Railways *by Alan A. Jackson (David & Charles)*

London's Historic Railway Stations *by John Betjeman and John Gay (John Murray)*

BR Steam Motive Power Depots, LMR/SR/WR *by Paul Bolger (Ian Allan)*

London Steam in the Fifties *by Brian Morrison (Ian Allan)*

Railways of the Southern Region *by Geoffrey Body (Patrick Stephens Ltd)*

Railways of the Western Region *by Geoffrey Body (Patrick Stephens Ltd)*

LMS Engine Sheds, Vols 1 and 2 *by Chris Hawkins & George Reeve (Wild Swan)*

LMS Reflections *by Bob Essery & Nigel Harris (Silver Link)*

The West London Joint Railways *by J. B. Atkinson (Ian Allan)*

Jowett's Railway Atlas *by Alan Jowett (Patrick Stephens Ltd)*

Rail Atlas - Great Britain & Ireland *by S. K. Baker (Oxford Publishing Co)*

The Railmag Index *by P. J. Long (P. J. Long)*

NORTH ACTON: Apart from the station canopy having been lengthened, North Acton station remains relatively unaltered - even the fire buckets are still evident - from when it was photographed on 24 June 1956 as '5700' Class 0-6-0PT No 7791 scuttles towards Old Oak Common depot with a short van train. The lines on the far right from Paddington to High Wycombe, via Acton Wells, no longer see expresses to Birkenhead, but are still used for freight and the occasional special working or main-line diversion. The freight line into Old Oak Common, in the centre of the picture, has, however, long since vanished, although since the 'present' scene was recorded on 4 February 1990, one track has been reclaimed by London Underground in connection with its Central Line modernisation programme. *Brian Morrison/Ken Brunt*

INTRODUCTION

As the railway network of Greater London is so extensive, two books in the 'British Railways Past and Present' series have been necessary in order to provide a reasonable coverage. This is the second volume, covering the western side of the capital together with the inner suburbs of Surrey, parts of Middlesex and a very small portion of Hertfordshire and Buckinghamshire, (these counties will be fully covered in other volumes). The lines from King's Cross, Liverpool Street and the Southern's Thames-side termini of Charing Cross, Cannon Street and Blackfriars, etc, are depicted in 'Past and Present' No 7, with this book concentrating upon the environs of Paddington, Marylebone, Waterloo, Victoria, Euston and St Pancras, together with the West London Line and the western section of both the North and South London Lines.

Many of the 'past' photographs are from the 1950s and are from my own collection, but a number of important gaps in my own coverage of the area have been kindly filled by fellow railway photographers Brian Beer, Stanley Creer and Philip J. Lynch; and for the remainder I am indebted once more to Dick Riley, who has again allowed me the pick of his extensive collection - like the well-known lager advertisement, Dick really did find parts that others failed to reach!

In the 1950s the British Railways Board was not averse to issuing lineside access permits to railway photographers who had their work published in the magazines of the day, and this facility allowed the use of vantage points such as signal boxes and signal gantries which, today, no longer exist. It is for this reason that the desired elevation could not be achieved for a few of the present-day views. Similarly, embankments were kept well cut back in steam days, but with the advent of modern diesel and electric traction the risk of fire from hot cinders has been eliminated. In just one or two instances the spread of nature has made an exact location copy difficult, or even impossible.

The changes which have occurred to the railway termini on the western side of London over the past four decades have, in some instances, been minimal; apart from the advent of overhead electrification, St Pancras remains substantially unaltered, whereas Euston station has been totally rebuilt. Building development at Victoria has visually changed some parts of the station but not others, while the main body of Waterloo is virtually unchanged even though drastic engineering works envelop the Windsor Lines platforms in readiness for a new international terminal for Channel Tunnel traffic. Marylebone has been extensively modernised and now utilises only two of the original three roof sections. The track layout at Paddington has been rationalised but, apart from modernisation of the concourse and renovation of the magnificent roof, Brunel's famous train shed is unchanged, and the unsightly signs of overhead electrification have still to arrive. Of the lines radiating out from these stations, differences between 'past' and 'present' are equally diverse, and branch lines such as Brentford, Merton Abbey, Staines West and Uxbridge Vine Street have vanished altogether.

The fate of the capital's famous West London steam sheds is variable in the extreme. Old Oak Common is still a major depot for diesel traction of all types, albeit with an uncertain long-term future, and Willesden houses and maintains the majority of the electric motive power for the West Coast Main Line services. Stewarts Lane looks after Intercity's 'Gatwick Express' locomotives and stock, in addition to diesel locomotives for both Network SouthEast Sector's Civil Engineers and Railfreight Sector, and stables large numbers of Southern EMUs. Cricklewood, Camden Town, Kentish Town and Nine Elms, however, have gone, together with the outlying depots of Slough, Neasden and Feltham; Southall remains as a haven for preserved steam, but with a much reduced capacity. The old LSWR shed at Strawberry Hill has been given modern importance, and Wimbledon continues to care for the suburban electric units which ply their trade on South Western Line services to and from Waterloo.

Apart from the photographers already mentioned, thanks are in order to a number of British Rail personnel who have been kind enough to provide facilities to duplicate some of the photographs which had to be taken from within their boundary fences and, as with the first London volume, to Derek Mercer, who again undertook most of the printing from both old and new negatives, his expertise remaining undiminished.

In the first London volume thanks were also given to the manufacturers of steel ladders, heavy-duty denim trousers, sturdy boots, sticking plasters and insect bite ointment. No lesser thanks are due once again to them following many forays into Western London.

Brian Morrison

Paddington

PADDINGTON (1): Despite the main concourse (or 'the Lawn' as it is known) being deepened to accommodate modern arrival and departure indicator displays, with a corresponding reduction in platform lengths, and despite the extensive renovations being carried out on the station, particularly to the roof, Brunel's great Paddington train shed has changed hardly at all since it was completed in 1854, except for additions and a few alterations brought about by traffic volume. At platforms 9 and 10 on 24 March 1951, 'Castle' Class 4-6-0 No 4096 *Highclere Castle* has brought in empty coaching stock to form an express for Bristol Temple Meads, while 'King' 4-6-0 No 6005 *King George II* approaches the buffer-stops with the 07.30 train from Shrewsbury.

At the same spot on 13 April 1992, Class '47/4' No 47636 *Sir John de Graeme* and Class '43' 'Intercity 125' power car No 43169 *The National Trust* make an extreme motive power contrast with, respectively, morning arrivals from Oxford and Bristol Temple Meads. The style of taxi has also changed somewhat! *Both BM*

PADDINGTON (2): Looking towards the buffer-stops from the country end of Paddington station, nothing of note has altered over the years apart from the motive power and coaching stock, and a change from bullhead rail to the modern flat-bottom variety - and there is a lot more rubbish in evidence! Shortly before withdrawal in 1953, the last Churchward 'Saint' Class 4-6-0 No 2920 *Saint David* waits to leave platform 4 with a special working for Swindon, the first coach of which was part of the GWR 'Centenary' stock introduced in 1935 for the 'Cornish Riviera Limited' and 'Bristolian' expresses.

At the same position on 14 May 1990, the 19.35 High Speed Train (HST) service for Penzance prepares to depart with Class '43' 'Intercity 125' power car No 43023 *County of Cornwall* providing appropriate front end traction. *Stanley Creer/KB*

PADDINGTON (3): 'Castle' Class 4-6-0 No 5042 *Winchester Castle* approaches Paddington hauling an express from Cheltenham Spa on 1 June 1951, and passes the goods depot constructed on the site of the very first Paddington station.

Some 40 years later, the 14.15 local service from Reading is seen at the same position and is formed of Network SouthEast Sector-liveried Class '117' three-car DMU No L429. The lower portion of the goods depot brick wall remains but the 'Virol' sign has gone! The backdrop to the scene is now the elevated Westway approach to the M40 motorway. *Both BM*

RANELAGH BRIDGE: Apart from an occasional change of paint colour, the series of massive iron girder road bridges which span the lines into Paddington have not been altered since their construction. The same cannot be said for the track layout, however, which has been drastically 'rationalised'. On 3 August 1958 the 11.55 train for Pembroke Dock passes beneath Ranelagh Bridge in the charge of 'Hall' Class 4-6-0 No 4991 *Cobham Hall*.

As can be observed from the building to the rear of Ranelagh Bridge, this September 1989 scene was photographed from exactly the same standpoint, but the track on which *Cobham Hall* was travelling has been lifted. However, the lineside cabin is still intact, as the 16.10 service for Oxford commences its journey from Paddington powered by 'Class 47/7' No 47714 in Network SouthEast (NSE) livery with matching stock. *Both BM*

RANELAGH BRIDGE DEPOT: To avoid the necessity of constant trips back and forth to Old Oak Common Motive Power Depot (MPD) for fuelling purposes, locomotives which arrived at Paddington were able to re-fuel at nearby Ranelagh Bridge depot, a short distance down the line. The advent of HST services, however, removed nearly all locomotive haulage from Intercity working diagrams, and the fuelling point was no longer considered necessary. With classes '47', '50' and '52' prevalent, the fuelling point on 21 May 1975 was a busy place.

By September 1989, however, the whole area was derelict, and since this photograph was taken has been made into a car park. *Both BM*

WEST LONDON SIDINGS: Situated between Ladbroke Grove and Old Oak Common, West London Sidings were once a hive of activity with continuous shunting in progress to form goods and van trains of varying types. 'Castle' Class No 5094 *Tretower Castle* passes on 19 October 1957, hauling the 14.15 train for Worcester.

An 'Intercity 125' unit, with Class '43' power car No 43182 leading, forms the 10.25 Paddington-Paignton HST on 25 February 1990. Apart from the white building above the train, the scene today is barely recognisable. *R. C. Riley/BM*

Old Oak Common (81A)

OLD OAK COMMON YARDS: With a typical rake of suburban stock of the period in tow, '6100' Class Prairie tank No 6127 heads a Paddington-bound local service past Old Oak Common yards on 29 August 1959, and passes the new signal box under construction at the time (on the left) to replace the one opposite.

On 15 April 1989, the same scene shows the signal box (now nearly 30 years old), 'rationalisation' of permanent way, and empty space where the sidings used to be. A three-car Class '117' DMU No L412 forms the 11.30 stopping train from Maidenhead to Paddington, and Class '50' No 50037 *Illustrious* passes outbound with the 12.15 Paddington-Oxford 'Network Express'. Since this view was recorded, the tracks in the foreground which formed the spur up to North Pole Junction on the West London Line (see pages 34/5) have been removed to make way for the construction of North Pole International service depot to be used for Channel Tunnel stock. *R. C. Riley/BM*

OLD OAK COMMON SHED (I): Opened in 1906 and closed for steam traction in 1965, Old Oak Common Traction & Rolling Stock Maintenance Depot today is still a busy place, with two main sections, one for maintenance and repair of diesel locomotives and the other for maintenance of 'Intercity 125' units and DMUs. Outside the Repair Shop (which is still known locally as 'the Factory') on a miserable 21 November 1954, heavy repairs are under way on 'Castle' 4-6-0 No 5077 *Fairey Battle*, seen minus tender and a pair of driving wheels.

Outside 'the Factory' on Old Oak Common's Open Day of 17 August 1991 is paraded Class '50' No 50050 (restored to original livery with number D400), Class '47/4' No 47484 *Isambard Kingdom Brunel*, Class '31/5' No 31568 *The Enginemen's Fund*, and preserved Class '35' 'Hymek' No D7018. *Both BM*

OLD OAK COMMON SHED (2): No interior view of the shed at Old Oak could really convey its size. A lesser-known Churchward masterpiece, it comprised four 28-road roundhouses under one overall roof and was claimed by the Great Western Railway to be the largest of its type in the world. On 20 March 1955, fitted with condensing gear for working over the London Transport Metropolitan Line, Class '5700' 0-6-0 Pannier tank No 9706 rests inside one of the roundhouses.

Little remains of the 444 ft x 360 ft building today, and a car is parked where once the Pannier tank stood. The Class '08' shunter No 08454 rattling past would have been outside the original wall. *Both BM*

OLD OAK COMMON SHED (3): Seen alongside the shed office building on 5 May 1956, 'King' Class 4-6-0 No 6011 *King James I*, fitted with a double chimney, has the chalked legend on its smokebox door 'Brum O Man U 5'!

In somewhat altered form, and minus chimneys, the old building still exists today, but the adjoining blackened steam shed has been replaced by a three-road fuelling depot which, on 27 January 1990, contained a Class '08' shunter. *BM/KB*

Westward from Paddington

WEST EALING: Steaming freely through West Ealing on 10 August 1957, '4700' Class 2-8-0 No 4700 itself heads for the West Country with the 12.05 train from Paddington to Kingswear.

By 11 March 1992 the sidings have been sold off for business development, various buildings have sprung up in the background and the blackened station has received a welcome facelift. One of Intercity Sector's long-range-fuel-tank Class '47/4s', No 47826, scurries past with the 09.18 Brighton-Glasgow Central service, the 'Sussex Scot'. *R. C. Riley/BM*

SOUTHALL (1): Approaching Southall with a down goods train off the Brentford Dock branch on 10 August 1957, Class '5700' 0-6-0PT No 9641 passes its home shed of Southall; it carries the appropriate 81C shedplate on its smokebox door. Closed to passenger services in May 1942, the line remains open to the present day for freight only, but not as far as the old docks.

Coming off the branch with the 08.12 Sunday refuse train from Brentford Town Yard to Appleford waste processing plant on 11 February 1990 is Class '56' No 560038, rather inappropriately bearing *Western Mail* nameplates. *R. C. Riley/BM*

SOUTHALL (2): Hammering non-stop through Southall station on 5 May 1956, 'Castle' Class 4-6-0 No 5029 *Nunney Castle* (now preserved and restored for main-line running) heads for Paddington with an express from Bristol Temple Meads.

With the down-side platform buildings removed, and those on the up side having been rebuilt and shortened, a pair of NSE-liveried Class '50s', Nos 50023 *Howe* and 50035 *Ark Royal*, provide super-power for the 09.30 Oxford-Paddington train on 11 February 1990. *BM/KB*

SOUTHALL SHED (81C): The first engine shed at Southall opened in 1884. It was closed for steam in 1965, but remained open for the maintenance of diesel traction for a further three years, after which it stayed as a stabling point until 1986. Outside the eight-road shed on 11 June 1965 'Castle' Class 4-6-0 No 7029 *Clun Castle* is decorated with a GWR coat of arms ready to haul the 16.15 Paddington-Banbury train, the last regularly-scheduled steam working from the London terminus - 127 years after the broad-gauge *North Star* departed with the first passenger train.

Although the smoke outlet chimneys have been removed and the rails are becoming overgrown, the shed building remains intact, the premises now being used by the steam preservation movement as a London base for main-line steam. On 15 April 1989 Class '43' power car No 43191 *Seahawk* rushes past behind the fuelling bay, leading an 'Intercity 125' HST which is forming the 17.45 service from Paddington to Penzance. *Brian Beer/BM*

BRENTFORD DOCK: Under the auspices of the Great Western & Brentford Railway, the branch line from Southall to Brentford Dock had its beginnings in broad gauge days, opening for goods traffic on 18 July 1859, and for passengers on 1 May 1860. First leased to, and later vested in, the GWR, standard gauge was added in 1861, and by 1956 the combined merchandise and coal both forwarded and received totalled some 200,000 tons. '5700' Class 0-6-0PT No 8750 shunts the dock in March 1958.

The dock closed on the last day of 1964 and has since been developed as a marina, encircled by residential properties although, as mentioned on page 21, part of the branch remains open to serve Brentford Town Yard refuse transfer centre. However, passenger services, which were never of any particular significance, ceased in 1942, and it is reported that the last train was actually hauled by an unlikely class of locomotive, a 'Dean Goods' 0-6-0. *R. C. Riley/BM*

UXBRIDGE VINE STREET was the first GWR branch line in the London area and was solely broad gauge until 1871. It was also the first of the town's three stations, opening in 1856, and until 1904 enjoyed a monopoly of the town's rail transport. On 20 July 1952 the West Drayton & Yiewsley auto-train stands at the buffer-stops.

When the London Passenger Transport Board opened a new and spacious station in the High Street in 1938, the GWR's Vine Street station received a blow from which it never recovered; the final demise of passenger services came on 10 September 1962, with cessation of freight traffic on 13 July 1964. The site today is a car park for Post Office employees, with the modern building of Charter House in the background housing the head office of the Coca-Cola & Schweppes organisation. Although one platform face can still be discerned on the right, one could say that Vine Street station has been 'schwepped' away! *R. C. Riley/KB*

STAINES WEST: The single-line branch from West Drayton to Staines West opened to Colnbrook in August 1884, reaching Staines on 2 November of the following year. The line was a rural one, and passengers from the intermediate station of Yeoveney (initially Runnymede) were required to signal to the train driver to stop. Latterly a diesel railcar was used for passenger traffic, but when this photograph of the auto-train was taken on 20 July 1952 motive power was in the hands of '1400' Class 0-4-2T No 1462, which still shows the legend 'GWR' on the tanksides.

Passenger services to Staines West ceased in March 1965, but part of the line still remains open for freight traffic to Thorney Mill stone terminal, the remainder having been closed in 1991 when the Colnbrook oil terminal to the north of the station was no longer required. A line of tanks at the now closed oil terminal can just be discerned above the parked cars in the 1990 scene, with one track and both station wall and platform still in evidence. *R. C. Riley/BM*

IVER: On 27 May 1956, '6100' Class 2-6-2T No 6140 restarts a Paddington-bound local train from Iver.

Nearly 34 years on, the scene has hardly altered except for the elimination of the telegraph poles and the growth of a tree. Passing at speed through the station on 10 March 1990, Class '47/3' No 47315, in 'general-user' grey livery, powers the 10.00 Newbury-Paddington 'Network Express'. Calling at all stops, the steam-hauled services from Reading took a little under two hours for the journey to Paddington. Today a first-generation DMU is expected to cover the same schedule in around 1¹/₄ hours. The advent of new Class '165/1' 'Thames Turbo' stock is scheduled to further reduce the journey to under the hour. *R. C. Riley/BM*

SLOUGH: A precursor of the 'Intercity 125' HSTs, one of the Metro-Cammell-built 'Blue Pullman' sets forms the 'Bristol Pullman' from Paddington on 10 October 1963, sweeping through Slough with semaphore signals indicating a clear road ahead.

Although a number of background buildings survive, indications of a diminishing railway dominance abound as the modern HST counterpart is seen at the same spot on 10 March 1990, forming the 12.00 Paddington-Swansea service. *R. C. Riley/KB*

West London Line

CHELSEA & FULHAM: The West London Extension Railway was opened on 1 April 1863, as a partnership between the LNWR, GWR, LSWR and LB&SCR, who, between them, formed the West London Joint Railways. The first station on the north bank of the River Thames was Chelsea & Fulham, which in company with the rest of the line lost its passenger services in the early days of the Second World War, on 20 October 1940. At the end of hostilities, the Joint Railways were unable to restore services as enemy bombing had badly damaged and even obliterated some stations and, in any event, the prospect of Nationalisation loomed and they were not prepared to spend money on repairs. On 6 February 1955, the station still stood but was demolished shortly afterwards.

Today the forecourt is a car park for a block of flats, and the railway is out of sight behind the brick wall. The background buildings on the left, however, appear unchanged. *R. C. Riley/BM*

CREMORNE VIADUCT: Dating from the opening of the West London Extension Railway in 1863, Cremorne Viaduct spans Chelsea Creek and takes its name from the once-famous pleasure gardens and pier which stood at the location. The viaduct was designed by the Chief Engineer to the LNWR, William Boker, and built in cast iron segments to compliment the style of other River Thames railway bridges. The trackbed was constructed to broad-gauge dimensions at the extra expense of the GWR, but little use was made of the third rail after the first few years. Popularly known today as Chelsea Bridge, the structure has six 120-foot-span arches over the water, and is 1,020 feet in length. On 27 December 1985, a Class '47' locomotive crosses the River Thames hauling the 09.58 Manchester Piccadilly-Brighton cross-country Intercity train.

Just over two years later, on 22 January 1988, Class '33/2' No 33204 is seen at the same place hauling a rake of EMU stock from Ilford Depot to Eastleigh Works for repair. In such a short period of time, what a difference to the surroundings! *Brian Beer/BM*

KENSINGTON OLYMPIA (1): At the end of the Second World War Kensington Addison Road station buildings were in a very poor state and were eventually dismantled in 1958. The south-west bay was rebuilt to accommodate London Transport's District Line trains and a new, small, station building was constructed on the site of the original down-side building and opened on 24 May 1966. At the same time a new 'Motorail' terminal shed was built on the site of the old north-west bay, but this was later abandoned and is now a car park. The station was renamed Kensington Olympia in 1946, when London Transport's special trains for Olympia exhibitions and the like commenced. On 20 August 1955 the 12.30 Hastings-Manchester train passes Kensington Middle box behind Class 'H2' 'Brighton Atlantic' No 32424 *Beachy Head*.

Kensington Olympia was given the status of an Intercity station when the Sector's 'Cross-London' services commenced in 1986, but these have not been the success anticipated and have since been severely reduced. The trains remaining still stop here, however, and the station is also still used by the peak-hour shuttle from Clapham Junction, popularly known as the 'Kenny Belle'. On 29 July 1989 a through passenger service again used the centre tracks when the 08.30 Victoria-Worcester 'Venice-Simplon Orient Express' (VSOE) special passed, hauled by Class '47/4' No 47828. Middle box and the majority of the semaphore signals have long since disappeared. *R. C. Riley/KB*

KENSINGTON OLYMPIA (2): Approaching the station and passing Kensington North Main box, 'Schools' Class 4-4-0 No 30915 *Brighton* hauls London Midland Region maroon stock forming the 11.05 Walsall-Hastings service on 22 August 1959.

Only Kensington South signal box remains at the present time, both North and Middle boxes having been demolished. Passing the same location on 7 June 1991 Class '60' No 60045 *Josephine Butler* works 'light engine' back to Stewarts Lane Depot. Just one re-positioned semaphore signal remains, the houses backing on to the line are now shielded by a little more foliage, and a roof extension has been built on to one of them. *R. C. Riley/Brian Beer*

33

NORTH POLE JUNCTION: Situated south of Mitre Bridge Junction (which provides the connection between the West London Line and the West Coast Main Line at Willesden), North Pole Junction connected the West London Line with the former GWR main line at Old Oak Common (see page 15). On 31 August 1957 another action study of the handsome 'Brighton Atlantic' No 32424 *Beachy Head* is provided, as it steams past the signal box hauling the 12.35 cross-country train from Leicester to Hastings.

At the same position on 15 April 1989 Class '47/4' No 47466 hauls train 1Z37, the 09.56 'Footex' special for Wanderers supporters from Wolverhampton to Aldershot for a cup game. Apart from a few lineside accoutrements which have appeared, plus the loss of the signal box name, the only other changes at this location at the time related to the track layout, which was simplified in 1969 by merging the down line to Old Oak Common with the up line for a short distance with a facing crossover; the track on the left, which went to the former GWR carriage depot, was lifted at the same time. In order to clear the way for Channel Tunnel carriage sidings, the junction has now been taken out of use, but the signal box remains to control Mitre Bridge Junction, whose own signal box has been demolished. *R. C. Riley/KB*

Waterloo

WATERLOO (1): The original 1848 Waterloo station was located where platforms 7 to 11 are today, and was a modest terminus for the LSWR, taking over from the original Nine Elms station which had opened ten years earlier. Like Topsy, the station grew and grew; today it is the biggest station on British Rail, covering over 24l acres, and was opened in its present form by Queen Mary in 1922. In 1953 problems were being experienced with the Southern Region's Bulleid 'Pacifics'; Gresley Class 'V2' 2-6-2s were borrowed from the Eastern Region for a short period and worked a number of services from Waterloo, including the prestigious 'Bournemouth Belle', here waiting to leave behind No 60896 on 20 May 1953.

Very extensive engineering works in connection with the Waterloo International terminal for Channel Tunnel trains commenced in 1990 and have resulted in the Windsor Lines platforms, which dated from 1860, being totally demolished. The new international station, however, requires much longer platforms than the edifice it is replacing and the total acreage of the complete station upon completion of the work will be even greater than before. Wessex expresses today are operated by the impressive-looking 'Class 442' 5WES EMUs. On 26 July 1990 No 2417 awaits departure time with the 10.32 train for Weymouth. A number of changes to the platform canopies are self evident, and the exterior of the station building itself is now considerably brighter following belated removal of post-war grime. *R. C. Riley/BM*

WATERLOO (2): All of London's termini were somewhat dark and forbidding for quite a long period after the Second World War, and indeed for a number of years following Nationalisation. Eventually boarded roofs were replaced with glass again, and what glass still remained was cleaned. Although the steam days scene was taken after dark, the difference between the two views taken of platform 11 and separated by more than 39 years is quite marked - and would not have been very different had they both been taken during daylight hours! On Leap Year Day 1952 'West Country' 'Pacific' No 34011 *Tavistock* awaits departure with an evening train for Basingstoke.

On 5 February 1992, two five-car Class 442 'Wessex Electrics', Nos 2412 and 2418, form the 10.32 for Weymouth and the 10.45 for Poole respectively. *Both BM*

WATERLOO (3): Trackwork into Waterloo station has been rationalised as far as possible during the years which have passed between the dates of these two views, but the approach roads inevitably remain complicated in view of the number of platforms which require to be served. On 28 June 1952 'Lord Nelson' Class 4-6-0 No 30865 *Sir John Hawkins* arrives with a summer extra from Bournemouth, as another Bournemouth train departs.

With the Red Lion pub building still remaining on the left, but with a block of flats now occupying the right background, 'Wessex Electric' No 2423 forms a train from Poole on 26 July 1990. *Both BM*

WATERLOO (4): Apart from the numbering, the 'Windsor Lines' platforms 16 to 21 gave arriving passengers the impression that this section of Waterloo was a station in its own right, as it was not possible to cross from platform 16 to platform 15 without first passing through the barrier and entering again on the other side of a wall. Also the spandrels of the cast iron columns supporting the glass roof were unlike anything in the main body of the station; in fact they dated from 1885, when what was first known as the 'North Station' was added. Probably due to its detachment from the rest of the station, the area of the 'Windsor Lines' platforms was chosen for the site of Waterloo International terminus for Channel Tunnel trains. Before total demolition commenced, all three types of Class '455' EMU were on view at the platforms on 20 June 1988, with Class '455/7' No 5722 forming the 12.43 for Windsor & Eton Riverside, Class '455/9' No 5906 working the 12.45 for Kingston, and Class '455/8' No 5873 having just arrived as the 11.23 from Woking via Hounslow.

At the same location on 3 May 1992 some semblance of order is beginning to return as the International station takes shape after two years of being nothing more than a very large hole containing a myriad of building works. *Both BM*

WATERLOO (5): Work on the LSWR's underground line from Waterloo to Bank station in the heart of the City of London, the Waterloo & City Railway, commenced in 1894, was completed in 1898, and was a very successful alternative to the fleet of two-horse buses which had previously carried commuters from Waterloo to Bank! Known to nearly everyone as 'the Drain', the Waterloo & City Railway runs beneath the River Thames on double track, and today the journey of 1 mile 1,012 yards is scheduled to take 6 minutes. One of the original Dick Kerr & Company single motor cars constructed in 1899 for off-peak services on the railway was photographed at Waterloo in November 1940.

The present-day view shows Class '487' stock built in the same year of 1940 by English Electric and now painted into NSE livery. As indicated by the advertisement on the tunnel wall, after a life of over 50 years this stock is now scheduled for replacement. The end of the lattice-work footbridge can just be glimpsed beyond the modern cladding in the top left-hand corner of the photograph. *C. J. Marsden Collection/BM*

41

WATERLOO (6): Forming the 13.58 service for Reading, Class '423' 4VEP No 7745 leads another unit of the same class away from the 'Windsor Lines' platforms on 11 June 1985.

With the modernistic structure of Waterloo International station taking shape in the background, Channel Tunnel trains will soon be using this part of the station, work having commenced in 1990 with the demolition of Waterloo signal box and the construction of a giant raft to widen the station 'throat'. The comparison between these two views makes it evident that the term 'past' is merely relative! *Both BM*

VAUXHALL: Originally known as Vauxhall Bridge, the station here opened on the same day as Waterloo, its four island platforms being built on a viaduct with stairway connections to the roads below. Until 1910 all trains for Waterloo were stopped here for tickets to be collected by a veritable army of railway staff, known to the passengers of the day as 'the Vauxhall Mob'! On 4 May 1957 'King Arthur' Class 4-6-0 No 30454 *Queen Guinevere* was photographed from the London end of the platforms heading a Waterloo-Basingstoke train.

On 31 May 1990 the track layout appears to have changed very little, but the background houses have vanished and the office blocks on the north side of the line have been extended. Class '455/9' EMU No 5901 brakes for the station stop, forming the 13.55 local service from Waterloo to Hampton Court. *Both BM*

Nine Elms (70A)

LOCO JUNCTION: On 6 September 1958 'Merchant Navy' 'Pacific' No 35021 *New Zealand Line* passes beneath Loco Junction signal box as it backs down to Waterloo to pick up stock. All locomotive movements between the main line and Nine Elms shed were controlled by this box, which spanned the tracks until the depot closed in 1967.

The view on 25 March 1990 had to be taken from over the barbed wire fencing erected around what is now the site of the New Covent Garden Market, and shows a Waterloo-Portsmouth Harbour EMU express working with 4BEP Class '412' No 2303 leading a 4CIG unit. Apart from the running tracks, nothing whatever appears to remain from the original scene, and Loco Junction is a junction no more. *R. C. Riley/KB*

STEWARTS LANE CHORD: Passing the site of the old Nine Elms complex on 7 June 1987, Class '73/1' electro-diesel No 73142 *Broadlands* powers the 10.34 (Sun) Weymouth-Waterloo service between Queenstown Road and Vauxhall stations.

Less than four years later the modernistic lighting standard to illuminate the Covent Garden Market car park remains to dominate the foreground, but the signal gantry has been moved and, in the background, construction of the new viaduct carrying the Stewarts Lane Chord is nearly complete. The chord links the classic Dover-Victoria route with South Western tracks, and will provide access for Channel Tunnel trains to Waterloo International station. Passing on 26 January 1992 is 'Pullman'-liveried Class '73/1' No 73101 *Brighton Evening Argus* hauling ECS from Clapham Yard to Waterloo. The locomotive was renamed *The Royal Alex'* at a ceremony at Brighton on 2 May 1992. *Both BM*

NINE ELMS SHED: After the closure of the original London & Southampton railway terminus of Nine Elms in 1848, three roads of the station were utilised as new running shed accommodation, a further six-road building being added a year later. These structures were replaced on the other side of the main line by a new seven-road through shed in 1865, and this in turn was superseded 11 years later by a spacious semi-roundhouse with access from two turntables. This sufficed for 20 years until a large 15-road straight shed was built alongside the roundhouse, forming the depot layout as it remained until closure in 1967. On 16 September 1968 Class 'H16' 'Pacific' tank No 30519 is seen on the depot in the position where the mobile hamburger and candy floss trader was to stand more than 20 years later providing fast food for customers to the New Covent Garden Sunday market. Currently nothing remains of the 70A shed site, it having been totally redeveloped as the new market complex. *Both BM*

South Western Lines

CLAPHAM JUNCTION (1): Situated at a point where the ex-LSWR lines from Waterloo meet the ex-LB&SCR lines from Victoria and the West London Joint Line to Kensington Olympia, Clapham Junction is proclaimed as 'Britain's Busiest Railway Station'. Actually situated some $1\frac{1}{4}$ miles from Clapham, the station was opened on 2 March 1863 in order to provide a convenient interchange between passengers of the three railway companies including those of the London Chatham & Dover Railway, which company had running powers from Factory Junction, on the Victoria-Herne Hill route, to Longhedge Junction. Rounding the curve through the station on the London-bound main line on 25 July 1956, BR Standard '5MT' 4-6-0 No 75075 hauls a Bournemouth West to Waterloo train, and passes Class 'E4' 0-6-2T No 32500 which is engaged in shunting stock in the adjacent yard.

Currently the scene is little changed, with modern-looking advertisement hoardings and lamp standards having replaced their 1950s counterparts, and the platform itself now looking rather the worse for the passage of many feet. Passing through is Class '421/5' 'Portsmouth Greyhound' 4CIG No 1305 leading the 13.06 'Network Express' from Portsmouth Harbour to Waterloo. *Both BM*

CLAPHAM JUNCTION (2): Clapham Junction's famous 'A' signal box was of LSWR design and dated from 1905. On 25 June 1951 'Merchant Navy' Pacific No 35005 *Canadian Pacific* propels the 15.54 Clapham Junction-Exmouth Junction empty milk tanks beneath the structure, prior to setting off via East Putney to the main line.

Stripped of its canopy and rebuilt, 'A' box was still in use on 31 May 1990 as Class '423/1' 4VEP No 3484 passed underneath forming the 14.50 train from Guildford to Waterloo.

The signalling centre at Wimbledon finally took over control of the main line out of Waterloo in April 1991, after which a gradual demolition of Clapham Junction 'A' box began. On 21 April 1992 just the gantry remains as Class '455/8' units Nos 5851 and 5830 pass, forming the eight-car 16.42 service from Windsor & Eton Riverside to Waterloo. *All BM*

CLAPHAM JUNCTION (3): Having traversed the West London Line, Stanier Class '8F' 2-8-0 No 48666 of Toton shed (18A) hauls a Willesden to Norwood freight up the sharp curve into platform 17 at Clapham Junction on 20 July 1951. Construction of a new power box is obscuring the view of LB&SCR-built Clapham 'B' box, while a concrete gantry has been erected in front of the semaphore signals to carry colour light 'starters' for the West London Line platforms.

On 2 June 1990 Class '47/4' No 47625 rolls into the same platform hauling the Saturday 07.25 'Intercity Holidaymaker' service from Manchester Piccadilly to Eastbourne. The 'new' power box is now itself out of use, while its predecessor 'B' box and its attendant signals are long gone. The colour lights are in place on their now blackened gantry, and the background buildings have changed out of all recognition. *BM/KB*

CLAPHAM CUTTING: Overtaking 4SUB electric units on suburban services from Victoria and Waterloo, Class 'S15' 4-6-0 No 30833 passes through Clapham cutting on 13 May 1963 with the 15.54 train from Waterloo to Basingstoke.

Apart from the drains having been covered over and a new signal gantry being in evidence, little appears to have changed in the intervening years to 23 February 1992, as a specially-powered 'Solent & Wessex Wanderer' railtour passes the same spot hauled by Class '56' No 56020 and Class '33/1' No 33116, the latter providing train heating. *Stanley Creer/BM*

DURNSFORD ROAD: Dating from the advent of electrification in 1915, sheds and repair shops were built by the LSWR at Durnsford Road, Wimbledon, together with a generating station which supplied the system. Passing the Power House on 2 March 1957 rebuilt 'Merchant Navy' 'Pacific' No 35014 *Nederland Line* is in charge of the down 'Bournemouth Belle'.

Eventually the requirement of additional capacity for longer trains and improved services necessitated renewal and modernisation of the power supply system, and Durnsford Road Power House became redundant when all the current needed was taken from the National Grid; the quite handsome structure was finally demolished in 1965. On 25 March 1990 the 16.25 Waterloo-Portsmouth Harbour express service passes the site, formed of Class '412' 4BEP No 2306 leading Class '421/2' 4CIG No 1219. With Durnsford Road sheds replaced in 1974 by today's double-ended 'Wimbledon Train Care' depot, nothing remains of the original scene except for the little brick-built lineside hut, and even that has lost its door! *R. C. Riley/KB*

WIMBLEDON PARK CARRIAGE SHEDS: With 4COR 'Nelson' EMUs as the majority occupants of Wimbledon Park sheds on 2 March 1957, a London Transport District Line train of red-liveried 'R' Stock passes on the approaches to Wimbledon station.

Apart from the change in rolling-stock and the demise of the Durnsford Road Power House chimneys, the scene is much the same on 25 March 1990 as silver-liveried District Line 'C69' Stock passes stabled Class '455s' and a Class '423' 4VEP. Although having been turned around and also having its door removed, the small hut still manages to remain in situ, albeit tilting rather ominously. *R. C. Riley/BM*

WIMBLEDON (1): Passing Wimbledon 'B' box on 2 March 1957, the 13.30 Waterloo to Bournemouth and Weymouth express is powered by grubby 'Merchant Navy' 'Pacific' No 35027 *Port Line*. Travelling in the opposite direction, heading towards Wimbledon station, a local train is formed of one of the many four-car suburban units (4SUBs) which then existed, No 4514.

On 25 March 1990 a Waterloo-Weymouth semi-fast service passes the same location with Class '421/2' No 1243 leading. The track has been rationalised, the background buildings have been supplanted by 'modern' commercial structures, and the only remaining sign of the signal box is a section of protective railing. *R. C. Riley/KB*

WIMBLEDON (2): In steam days Wimbledon Yard was a thriving place where any number of locomotives could be seen at any one time engaged in a variety of activities. As late as the early 1970s rolling-stock was stabled there, a degree of shunting was still carried out, and the yard was the starting point for some freight traffic. Inhabitants on 2 March 1957 include Class 'C2X' 0-6-0 No 32553 and a pair of Class 'QI' 0-6-0s, Nos 33017 and 33015.

By 23 June 1990 the BR Property Board had disposed of the site, which is now in private hands. *R. C. Riley/KB*

WIMBLEDON 'C' JUNCTION: Jointly promoted by the Railway Correspondence & Travel Society (RCTS) and the Stephenson Locomotive Society (SLS), the 'South Western Suburban Railtour' special train headed by a pair of Class '0298' 2-4-0WTs, Nos 30587 and 30585, trundles past Wimbledon 'C' Junction box on 2 December 1962, while an EMU heads southwards round the junction for Sutton, opened by the Southern Railway as late as 1929-30.

With the path alongside the railway now obscured by foliage, the siding taken out and, of course, the signal box removed, Class '50' No 50049 *Defiance* approaches Wimbledon on 23 June 1990 powering the 11.50 Exeter St Davids-Waterloo train. *R. C. Riley/BM*

MERTON ABBEY: Of the two loop lines between Tooting and Wimbledon, one travelled via Haydon's Road and still exists today. The other, via Merton Abbey, was initially justified by promise of freight traffic to the copper mills situated there. Both lines were operated jointly by the LB&SCR and LSWR, but the Merton Abbey line closed to passengers in March 1929 following the opening of London Underground's Northern Line, and Collier's Wood station in particular. The chord remained busy with freight until the junction at the Tooting end was severed in March 1934, after which the section was worked as a long siding from Merton Park. As late as 1960 there were still two daily return goods trains working the line with one on Saturdays, but increased use of road transport resulted in the final coal train running to Merton Abbey on 1 May 1975, the track being quickly taken up, thereafter. In latter years restricted excursion traffic was allowed to use the line as shown in the scene of Maunsell 'Q' Class 0-6-0 No 30545 at the site of Merton Abbey station with a Locomotive Club of Great Britain special.

Little sign of any railway existed on 25 March 1990. *Stanley Creer/BM*

RAYNES PARK station was opened on the site of Epsom Junction in October 1871, and is the junction for the Epsom line and the Chessington South branch via Motspur Park. At speed through the station on 30 July 1963, rebuilt Bulleid 'West Country' 'Pacific' No 34026 *Yes Tor* heads 12 well-laden coaches forming the 18.00 Waterloo-Plymouth express.

With the cables and their raised covering removed from the base of the signal box, together with the nameboard and the bush, Class '50' No 50005 *Collingwood* is caught in exactly the same position on 30 April 1990, racing past with the 17.34 'West of England' service from Waterloo to Yeovil Junction. The multiple-aspect colour light signals appear relatively unchanged over the years, whereas the platform lighting is obviously more effective! *P. J. Lynch/BM*

BERRYLANDS: Although situated on the main line with trains passing every few minutes throughout the day, only Hampton Court commuter services actually call at Berrylands, a station which was built in 1933 to serve inhabitants of local housing developments and actually lies on the portion of line which was elevated to cross Norbiton Common and the Hogsmill River. Passing through the station on 16 September 1961, 'Battle of Britain' 'Pacific' No 34069 *Hawkinge* makes haste for Waterloo with an express from Bournemouth.

On 21 February 1992, when the comparison photograph was taken, the multiple-aspect colour light gantry and the wooden-boarded platform appear unchanged, but the trees have grown somewhat, the platform lamps have been exchanged for examples of a newer type, and a chain-link fence takes the place of the old wooden palings. Powering the 09.45 'Network Express' from Exeter St Davids to Waterloo is Class '47/7' No 47710, named to assist in promoting the charity *Capital Radio's Help a London Child*. *Terry Gough/BM*

SURBITON station was opened by the London & Southampton Railway in 1838 and called Kingston, reflecting the railway's ambition to serve the town that successfully fought to keep it away - and has regretted it ever since! Before finally being accepted as Surbiton, the station carried the names Kingston Junction and then Surbiton & Kingston. It was resited seven years after opening, and completely rebuilt between 1936 and 1939. Here we have a second view of the 'South Western Suburban Railtour' of 2 December 1962 (see page 57) showing the Beattie 2-4-0WTs again (this time with No 30585 leading No 30587), departing from Surbiton and heading for Hampton Court Junction.

Today the once extensive goods yard and sidings are the official station car park, and a Sunday visit was necessary in order to avoid the comparison scene being almost totally obscured by cars. Taken from the same standpoint, Class '455/8' No 5857 moves away, forming a service for Hampton Court. *Stanley Creer/BM*

HAMPTON COURT BRANCH: The short branch line to Hampton Court station, situated on the south bank of the River Thames near Hampton Court Palace, first opened for horse traction in 1849, and was once proclaimed as 'the station for East and West Molesey'. Today the branch is operated almost exclusively by Class '455' units which ply their trade to and from London on a half-hourly basis, but there was a time when a steady diet of EMUs could be supplemented to some extent by the daily goods train, which used to be steam-hauled down the branch. On 16 December 1959 '700' Class 0-6-0 No 30699 was the engine in use.

Approaching its destination on 21 February 1992 is Class '455' No 5859 as the 10.55 from Waterloo, seen at the same position on the line but photographed nearer the tracks, the encroaching vegetation making a more accurate and wider view impossible. *Terry Gough/BM*

CHESSINGTON SOUTH: The last line to be constructed by the Southern Railway, the 4¹/₄-mile branch to Chessington South was intended to provide a railway service to new housing estates springing up south of Surbiton, but by the time the construction reached its present position the Second World War was imminent and precluded any further progress. Thereafter the 'Green Belt' effectively halted further housing developments in the area south of Chessington, and the original intention of continuing the line to Leatherhead never materialised. On Derby Day, 2 June 1954, the Royal Train left from Chessington South instead of the more usual Tattenham Corner station. Awaiting arrival of the Royal party is a suitably groomed 'West Country' 'Pacific', No 34011 *Tavistock*.

With the brick-built platform building now razed, and the opposite platform out of use, the 12.16 service for Waterloo awaits the appropriate time for departure, formed of Class '455/7' EMU No 5705. *BM/KB*

EPSOM: The present Epsom station site dates from 1859, although the railway first reached the town in 1847 when the London & Croydon Railway's Epsom Town station was opened. Epsom townsfolk enjoyed two stations until 1929 when the 'Town' closed, remaining open for freight only until 1965. On 25 March 1979 the distinctive 1928-dated Southern Railway overhead wooden signal box spanning the tracks was still in use and controlling the departure of Class '415/1' 4EPB No 5105 in the platform, forming the 14.12 Waterloo-Effingham Junction service.

Today Epsom commuters are almost spoilt for choice with their variety of services, and are able to travel direct to a choice of four London termini - Blackfriars, London Bridge, Victoria and Waterloo - using NSE's 'Thameslink', 'South Western Lines' and 'South London Lines' trains. On 21 February 1992 little has changed visibly at the location, although the signal box has lost its name since being taken out of use on 29 July 1990, when control was transferred to a new signalling centre at Wimbledon. The Class '455/9' EMU No 5907 in the platform has just arrived as the 13.18 train from Waterloo. *Both BM*

KINGSTON: Although the inhabitants of Kingston, and especially those with coaching interests, fought to keep the railway away from their town, and thus lost the opportunity to possess a main-line station in favour of nearby Surbiton, their present-day descendants enjoy four trains an hour to and from Waterloo, two Shepperton line services and two Kingston Loop trains via Strawberry Hill. The present-day station dates from a major reconstruction in 1934-35, prior to which the site comprised two levels, through lines at high level, and a terminus, known as Kingston Town, at street level; only the high level station now remains. Shunting the quite large Kingston goods yard on 4 June 1962 is Bulleid 'Austerity' Class 'Q1' 0-6-0 No 33011.

BR closed the yard in 1966, but the quite elaborate goods shed still stands and, on 5 February 1992, was in use for storage purposes by a company of bulk carriers; their lorry trailers now occupy the muddy yard.
Terry Gough/BM

PUTNEY: Served by Guildford and Windsor Line trains, in addition to those for the Kingston and Hounslow Loops, Putney is a busy station situated at the junction of Putney High Street and Richmond Road. Passing through the station on 15 August 1965 is the 'Western Ranger' railtour, organised by the Locomotive Club of Great Britain and powered by BR Standard Class '4MT' 4-6-0 No 75066.

With new buildings having replaced the rather ramshackle-looking ones on the south side of the line, and with a lot of the railway now shielded from view by trees, the 16.30 Waterloo-Reading service passes the same spot on 30 April 1990 formed of Class '423/1' 4VEP stock, Nos 3468 and 3428. *Stanley Creer/BM*

BARNES: The location of Barnes station dates from the opening of the line to Richmond in 1846, and it is presently well served by the majority of trains which call at Putney. The main station building is an elegant affair with tall chimneys and steep gables, but is partly obscured by the rather ugly platform canopy on the London-bound side. On 25 March 1962 a Waterloo-Kingston-Waterloo roundabout service restarts from the staggered platform formed of 4SUB EMU No 4385.

With one of the platform buildings demolished, and both Rocks Lane bridge and the station edifice nicely cleaned, present-day Class '455/8' EMU No 5865 forms the 16.05 Waterloo-Hounslow Loop service. *R. C. Riley/BM*

HOUNSLOW JUNCTION: The Hounslow Loop line was authorised to the Windsor, Staines & South Western Railway by an Act of 1847, with the provision of a service to Hounslow being one of its main objectives. The line runs from Barnes Junction to Hounslow Junction, and from there has connections to the Reading line via both Feltham and Whitton. On 30 April 1966 a special train organised by the RCTS returns from a visit to the Longmoor Military Railway and approaches Hounslow at Hounslow Junction, hauled by the last two Class 'U' 'Moguls' to be withdrawn from service, No 31791 piloting No 31639.

New houses and an abundance of foliage record the passage of time as Class '455/7' unit No 5701 passes the same location on 3 May 1990 forming the 14.20 train from Guildford to Waterloo. *Stanley Creer/BM*

Feltham (70B)

FELTHAM SHED (I): The final engine shed to be built by the LSWR, Feltham was completed in time for the Grouping of 1923, and was the first major depot in Great Britain to be constructed in concrete, setting a pattern upon which the Southern Railway would enlarge during the next 15 years. The six-road structure could hold 36 locomotives, which were essentially freight types used for hauling the variety of goods traffic generated from the large Feltham Hump Yards. The depot survived until the end of steam on the Southern Region, closing on 9 July 1967. The yards survived a few more years, but eventually succumbed to the run-down of wagonload freight. One of the many varieties of locomotive allocated to 70B was the '700' Class 0-6-0; No 30567 is depicted here outside the shed building on 21 May 1955.

An extensive area of wasteland now exists where once there was a hive of activity, and a wooden lighting post (the same one?) is the only remaining link between these two scenes. *BM/KB*

FELTHAM SHED (2): Running alongside the eastern end of Feltham shed was a single-ended repair bay, seen here with a Birmingham R&CW Type 3 diesel (later Class '33') and Classes 'Q1' and 'H16' steam locomotives outside. Amid the present-day wasteland scrub, just one wall of the building survives. *Lens of Sutton/KB*

North London Line

UPPER HOLLOWAY: Popularly known as the 'Tottenham and Hampstead' route, the present-day Gospel Oak to Barking line links the former Midland Railway and LNWR systems with those of the former Great Eastern and London, Tilbury & Southend companies. Over the years the line grew on a piecemeal basis, with the present-day western extremity to Gospel Oak opening in 1888 and being $12^1/_4$ miles from the eastern end of the railway at Barking. In addition to quite frequent cross-country freight trains, the route carries a Monday to Saturday half-hourly DMU service, connecting with Richmond-North Woolwich trains at Gospel Oak, and with LT&SR and LUL District Line trains at Barking. Approaching the Upper Holloway stop on 15 October 1984, the 14.45 train from Gospel Oak to Barking is formed of a two-car Birmingham RC&W Class 104 DMU.

On 30 April 1990 new industrial buildings have appeared alongside the line, and the Midland Railway signal box and its attendant semaphore signals have disappeared. In the siding is one of the few remaining Class '104' DMU units (now smartened up a little with NSE livery), and passing is a Pressed Steel Company Class '121' single car unit No 55030 forming the 12.45 Gospel Oak-Barking train. *Both BM*

GOSPEL OAK: As well as being the terminus for trains from Barking, Gospel Oak is an interchange for North Woolwich-Richmond services which operate every 20 minutes from Monday to Saturday, but strangely are not considered as being worth a Sunday service. In addition to these 'North London Lines' passenger trains, a considerable amount of freight traffic utilises the tracks through Gospel Oak Junction. Hauling a rake of empty HTV coal hoppers on 15 October 1984, Stratford-based Class '37s' Nos 37166 and 37044 head for home round the curve through the west end of the station.

A few months after the 'past' view was recorded the signal box was destroyed by fire, to be replaced in 1985 by the unlikely-looking wooden structure being passed on 4 April 1992 by Class '313' EMU No 313022 forming the 14.43 Richmond-North Woolwich train. Signalling is now of the multiple-aspect colour light variety, and the 'starter' is now situated behind the camera on the end of a now shortened platform. *Both BM*

HAMPSTEAD HEATH: At a time when trains from Richmond operated through Hampstead Heath and Gospel Oak to Broad Street terminus, Class '501' EMU No 501164 picks up speed again after the Hampstead Heath station stop on 15 October 1984, and heads for the now demolished City of London station (see 'British Railways Past and Present' No 7).

Following the demise of the Class '501' units, services on this line were in the hands of Southern Region Class '416/3' 2EPB EMUs for a period, but are now operated by the more modern Class '313' EMUs which were constructed in 1976-77. On 4 April 1992 No 313016 forms the 14.03 train from Richmond, which now travels the 22^1/$_4$ miles to North Woolwich in 1 hour 6 minutes, including no fewer than 26 stops! The lineside allotments are still in evidence, a small brick retaining wall has been built on the left, and the small lineside electrical box has received some unwelcome graffiti. *Both BM*

KENSAL GREEN JUNCTION: Situated between Kensal Rise station and Willesden, the junction at Kensal Green carries a large amount of cross-country freight traffic, in addition to the regular Richmond-North Woolwich passenger services. On 20 May 1984 Class '50' No 50032 *Courageous* passes with a train consisting mainly of empty Mk III sleeping cars from the overnight train from Penzance to Paddington, *en route* to Willesden for servicing at Willesden Carriage Depot (later known as Wembley Intercity Depot). The train reversed here at Kensal Green then, with the Class '25' on the other end leading, took the tracks on the extreme right to its destination, the devious routing being caused by a Sunday engineering possession.

Kensal Green Junction was remodelled and re-signalled in April 1985, rendering the signal box and semaphore signals redundant. On 4 April 1992 Class '33/0' No 33026 *Seafire* runs through the junction 'light engine', returning from Willesden Yard to the Southern Region. Again, a reversal has to be made here in order to take the line to the left which will gain access to home territory via Kew East Junction. Only one of the three background cooling towers now remains. *Brian Beer/BM*

ACTON WELLS JUNCTION: The North & South Western Junction Railway (N&SWJR) line from Willesden to Kew dates from 1853, and the focal point of the 3¾-mile line is Acton Wells Junction where five routes converge. From the north, there is the ex-N&SWJR line itself, the Midland line from Brent, and the route from Willesden High Level. From the south, the N&SWJR line runs to Kew, and a spur runs down alongside the ex-GWR main line into Acton Yard. From Kew, trains can diverge again either via Barnes or Brentford. On 4 May 1957 a transfer freight for Southern Region metals at Feltham passes the junction, hauled by ex-LSWR Urie Class 'H16' 'Pacific' tank No 30516.

Although the semaphore signals have been deposed by multiple-aspect colour light signalling, the ex-North London Railway Acton Wells Junction signal box, *circa* 1892, still controls the junction as, on 4 April 1992, USA-constructed Class '59/1' No 59101, later named *Village of Whatley*, passes with empty ARC hoppers from Allington, Kent, heading for the GWR main line and back to Whatley Quarry, via Acton. *R. C. Riley/BM*

Marylebone

MARYLEBONE (1): The Victorian visionary Sir Edward Watkin brought his Manchester, Sheffield & Lincolnshire Railway into London by its own difficult route, partly sharing the Metropolitan Railway's main line. He called it the Great Central Railway, and the first train steamed into the new terminus of Marylebone in March 1899. The Great Central Railway was the last main line to be constructed into London, and it was the first to disappear when all through services beyond the Chiltern Hills ceased on 3 September 1966, leaving the station with no trains beyond Aylesbury or Banbury. BR's Eastern Region continued local services until, after a brief spell of Western Region control, the London Midland Region was given the job of running down and overseeing an eventual closure. It was planned for High Wycombe trains to be diverted into Paddington, and for Aylesbury line travellers to be accommodated by a shuttle to Amersham, and thence to Baker Street. However, the advent of BR's Network SouthEast Sector in 1986, and its first Managing Director, Chris Green, in particular, brought about an upturn in Marylebone's fortunes which, today, has been completely modernised, both with regard to the refurbished station and its new trains.

The first view (above left) shows the station in 1981, when the train shed had three roof sections.

The same view on 28 February 1991 (left), during the refurbishment programme, shows only two of the three roof sections now remaining, and a Class '115' DMU departing as the 12.10 train for Aylesbury via Amersham.

The modern station is seen above on 22 March 1992, with Class '165/1' 'Chiltern Turbos' Nos 165011/024 departing as the 13.27 to High Wycombe, and others of the same class stabled in the new sidings on the right. *All BM*

MARYLEBONE (2): There was a time when Marylebone boasted a titled train, 'The Master Cutler' to Sheffield. On 5 July 1952 Class 'A3' 'Pacific' No 60052 *Prince Palatine* carries the appropriate headboard as it winds the service out of the terminus. Milk tank wagons working from the Shrewsbury area can be seen in the milk depot to the left.

Today the near tracks are used only to gain access to the train washer, and only the two far lines are used for incoming and outgoing traffic. On 19 March 1992 the 14.44 departure for Aylesbury is formed of a mish-mash of Class '115' DMU stock, with Driving Motor Brake Standard (DMBS) No 51655 leading. The background buildings and the bridge remain, but the milk tanks and the signal gantry are but memories past. *Both BM*

MARYLEBONE (3): In early 1962 four BR Standard 'Britannia' 'Pacifics' were allocated to Neasden shed and operated many of the main-line trains from Marylebone. Despite their somewhat run-down condition, three of them remained on the line until the depot closed, when they were transferred to Annesley. The class was then re-introduced to ex-GCR metals when eight were allocated to Banbury, and they saw out the last 12 months of Marylebone's main-line workings alongside the then new DMUs which were operating the suburban services. Retaining nameplates from happier days on the Scottish Region, No 70053 *Moray Firth* slugs up the 1 in 100 gradient out of the station on 5 February 1964, and approaches Lord's Tunnel with the 14.38 train to Nottingham.

In the same position, but heading towards the terminus, Class '165/0' No 165027 forms the 13.30 from Banbury on 19 March 1992. The background building still stands and, surprisingly, so does the lighting pole. *P. J. Lynch/BM*

Neasden (34E)

NEASDEN SHED: Opened by the Great Central in 1899, Neasden shed serviced and maintained locomotives for both Marylebone main-line and suburban trains, and in addition provided necessary facilities for motive power working into and from Neasden Yard. Probably the most cosmopolitan of all steam depots, engines from five different BR Regions could often be seen under the one roof. After Nationalisation, the depot was given the code 34E by the Eastern Region, but became 14D for the last four years of London Midland Region control when arrival of diesel units for the Marylebone suburban services resulted in closure in 1962. At about that time, with both engine allocation and staff transferred to Cricklewood (14A), the depot stands deserted.

No trace of the depot or the marshalling yards remains on 21 March 1992. *Lens of Sutton/BM*

Chiltern Lines

NORTHOLT JUNCTION (1): Fierce competition with the LNWR for passenger traffic between London and Birmingham led to a GWR requirement to shorten its lengthy route through Oxford. At the same time the GCR wanted an alternative access to London, as the Metropolitan Railway's lines were congested and the company uncooperative. Their common cause resulted in a new line being built from Old Oak Common through the Chilterns to High Wycombe and beyond. It was owned by the GWR as far as Northolt Junction, but thereafter came under the auspices of a GW&GC Joint Committee, incorporated in 1899. Running on the down line beneath the GWR main line to gain the Joint metals on 4 May 1957, Class 'Bl' 4-6-0 No 61028 *Unseke* heads for Manchester (London Road) with the 12.15 express from Marylebone.

On 24 February 1992 Class '165/0' 'Chiltern Turbo' No 165027 rounds the same curve forming the 12.40 service from Marylebone to Banbury. Trees have replaced the telegraph poles, and the encroaching foliage is looking rather menacing. *R. C. Riley/BM*

NORTHOLT JUNCTION (2): This quite remarkable and previously unpublished photograph shows 'King' Class 4-6-0 No 6020 *King Henry IV* hauling a relief to the 18.10 Paddington-Birkenhead express on 4 May 1957 passing Northolt Junction as the 18.20 Marylebone-Sheffield express passes beneath, hauled by Class 'A3' Pacific No 60107 *Royal Lancer*. It was certainly extremely lucky for the photographer that the two trains should pass this location at exactly the same time, but how many would have taken full advantage of the situation as Dick Riley has done here? The two trains did not, of course, collide at the converging junction ahead (where in any event there was quadruple track as far as West Ruislip), as the Sheffield one was travelling very slowly until it received a favourable signal!

Today exactly the same photographic vantage point is not available, but this view at the same location clearly shows the present state of the old GWR main line, where one of the two tracks is in process of being taken up, while the remaining one is rusted as a result of infrequent use; Birmingham traffic from Paddington has long since reverted to its circuitous route through Oxford. In the background a London Underground Central Line train of 1962 Stock passes, forming a service from Loughton to West Ruislip. *R. C. Riley/BM*

SOUTH RUISLIP: On FA Cup Final day, 1957, an up supporters' special working to Wembley is halted in South Ruislip station platform awaiting arrival of an Eastern Region guard for the run down the GC route into Wembley Hill station, while a Bicester-Paddington Army leave train passes on the through road. Both trains are worked by 'Hall' Class 4-6-0s, Nos 5927 *Guild Hall* and 6924 *Grantley Hall* respectively.

On 24 February 1992 the 12.30 Banbury-Marylebone service runs non-stop through the station formed of Class '165/0' No 165009, the '1' of the number having peeled off. The wooden platform shelter on the down side has been replaced with a glass box-like waiting room, the station building on the up side has been superseded by a like structure, and a new platform is evident, having been constructed over the old up slow line, leaving just the one through line instead of the original two. *R. C. Riley/BM*

DENHAM (I): Passing Denham West Junction signal box, and crossing the 181-yard viaduct over the Grand Union Canal to the south of Denham, '2251' Class 0-6-0 No 2290 hauls a goods train destined for Neasden Yard on 11 April 1953.

On 24 February 1992 'Chiltern Turbo' No 165006 forms the 10.45 service from High Wycombe to Marylebone and crosses the viaduct at the same point. Concrete sleepers and continuous rail replace the old bullhead variety, and there is no longer any trace of the semaphore signals and attendant signal box. *Both BM*

DENHAM (2): As late as 1960 12 express passenger workings from Paddington to Birmingham and beyond, and a number of semi-fast trains from Marylebone for the GW&GC Joint route via High Wycombe, still passed through Denham, together with the local services and the once-important through freight traffic, which has now virtually disappeared. On 11 April 1953 the 16.10 Paddington-Birkenhead express is powered through the station by 'Castle' Class 4-6-0 No 5008 *Raglan Castle*, and is photographed by the late Roy Wilson.

Apart the trains of household waste from Northolt to Calvert which currently operates at night, and the occasional weekend steam specials, the only remaining trains which can currently be observed at Denham are the 'Chiltern Line' local services, which are almost exclusively in the hands of the modern-looking Class '165/0' 'Chiltern Turbo' DMUs. Running into the station on 24 February 1992, No 165007 forms the 10.20 departure from Marylebone for High Wycombe. Both through lines have been taken up, and a number of other changes which have occurred over the years are readily discernible. *Both BM*

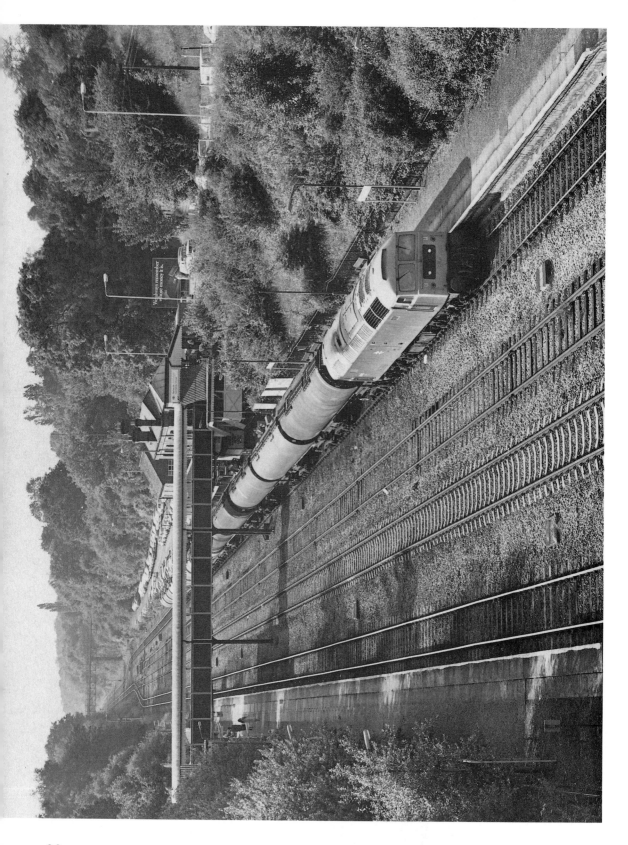

GERRARDS CROSS: Hauling the now-defunct train of bogie tanks from Thame to Ripple Lane, Barking, Class '47/0' No 47008 passes through the southbound platform road at Gerrards Cross on 3 July 1987.

With four tracks currently reduced to two by the expedient of building a new platform across the previous alignment, 'Chiltern Turbo' No 165026 restarts from the station forming the 09.55 semi-fast service from High Wycombe to Marylebone. *Brian Beer/BM*

NORTHWICK PARK: The first scheduled stop for BR trains from Marylebone to Aylesbury, via the ex-Great Central main line, is not reached until Harrow-on-the-Hill, intermediate stations being served by London Underground Ltd (LUL) sub-surface Metropolitan Line stock. Running beside the LUL lines at Northwick Park on 16 November 1963, the 14.38 Marylebone-Nottingham express working is hauled by 'Royal Scot' Class 4-6-0 No 46156 *The South Wales Borderer.*

With the first stop at Harrow-on-the-Hill approaching, the 15.10 Marylebone-Aylesbury train passes the same location on 27 February 1992, formed of a BR Derby-built Class '115' four-car DMU. The colour light signal and background rooftop can still be seen, and the chain-link fencing survives. The foreground field, however, is now the 'Jubilee Path', which some bushes are trying to shield from the railway. *P. J. Lynch/BM*

HARROW-ON-THE-HILL: The original station here was opened in 1880 as part of the Metropolitan Railway's 'extension' to Chesham and Aylesbury. When running powers to South Harrow Junction were obtained by the GCR, the station became part of the Metropolitan & GC Joint Line, and from 1899 passengers were able to travel into London by 'Metropolitan' services to Baker Street or to Marylebone on the Great Central trains. With suburban facilities into London inextricably linked, the station was rebuilt and expanded between 1938 and 1948, and passengers still have a choice of travelling by BR or London Underground services. On 28 July 1981, the 14.40 Aylesbury-Marylebone train restarts from the Harrow-on-the-Hill stop, formed of a four-car Class '115' DMU in three different liveries!

The same scene in 1992; the town of Harrow continues to grow, and Class '165/1' No 165022, in the latest version of NSE livery, leaves as the 13.39 service from Aylesbury to Marylebone. *Both BM*

NORTHWOOD HILLS: On 16 May 1964 the four-coach 14.38 Marylebone-Nottingham Victoria train passes Northwood Hills hauled by BR Standard '5MT' Class 4-6-0 No 73011.

There is always some trepidation when setting out to try and copy a picture from the past which includes a railway embankment in the foreground, as in so many cases the absence of attention to growth by both steam locomotive and BR employee over the years results in a reasonable duplicate of the scene being impossible. In most cases the location is discarded, and in the normal way this would have been the case here, but just one example of the problem was thought appropriate for this book! Behind the small woodland that has sprung up lineside at Northwood Hills, a Baker Street-Amersham Metropolitan Line train of LUL 'A' Stock passes the same location. *P. J. Lynch/BM*

Victoria

VICTORIA (1): The first Victoria station was opened by the LB&SCR in 1860, and allowed usage by the London Chatham & Dover Railway (LC&DR) until the latter's own adjoining terminus, shared with the GWR and its trains from Southall, was completed in 1862. Even after rebuilding was completed in 1909 the stations remained as separate entities, with their own individual entrances, platform numbers and station masters, and did not become one until 1924. The 'Chatham side' of Victoria consists of platforms 1 to 8, which, despite the extensive developments that have taken place above the 'air space' of the 'Central' portion of the station, remains relatively untouched by the passing years. On 4 April 1953 the 14.35 train for Ramsgate departs from platform 2, powered by 'Battle of Britain' 'Pacific' No 34072 *257 Squadron*, a locomotive which has been preserved and is still active today.

Showing headcode '14' for a Folkestone Harbour train travelling via Herne Hill and Bat & Ball, Class '411/5' 4CEP No 1550 awaits departure from the same platform on 7 April 1992. *R. C. Riley/BM*

VICTORIA (2): With only scars in the wall to show where Victoria (Eastern) signal box once stood, the same trains as shown on the previous page depart from Victoria on 4 April 1953 and 7 April 1992 respectively. The background buildings appear a mite cleaner, and two roof extensions have been built. Rather surprisingly, however, they appear otherwise to remain relatively untouched. *R. C. Riley/BM*

VICTORIA (3): Wearing the drab 'BR Corporate Blue' livery in which most locomotives were painted from the middle 1960s through the 1970s, Class '73/1' No 73140 departs from Victoria with the 'VSOE' bound for Folkestone Harbour.

With the eastern wall of the Victoria Place development above the 'Central' side of the station now providing the background, Class '411/5' 4CEP No 1513 departs from the same platform on 7 April 1992, forming the 10.23 service for Dover Priory. *Stanley Creer/BM*

Stewarts Lane (73A)

STEWARTS LANE SHED (I): The LC&DR Works Depot at Longhedge was established in the early 1860s, and the locomotive shed was rebuilt in 1881 from a half roundhouse to a straight shed. After the LC&DR merged with the South Eastern Railway in 1889 the premises became too small for the facilities required and the workshops were transferred to Ashford, Kent. The former erecting shop was retained for engine repairs to be carried out, and the carriage works became the carriage shed. Following closure of the ex-LB&SCR shed at Battersea Park, the Southern Railway further improved the depot, which was renamed Stewarts Lane in 1934, after the station of the same name which had been opened nearby by the LC&DR in 1863, but closed again just four years later. With Class 'E1' 4-4-0 No 31067 in the shed yard, the 'Golden Arrow' Pullman empty coaching stock from Victoria is brought into the depot for servicing on 18 August 1957 behind Class 'U' 'Mogul' No 31624. The stock is passing beneath the main line from Victoria, over which runs a six or eight-car rake of Class 2HAL EMU stock.

Nearly 30 years later the viewpoint has changed little, as a Class '411' 'Kent Coaster' EMU passes, forming a Victoria-Folkestone Harbour boat train. *R. C. Riley/BM*

STEWARTS LANE SHED (2): Prior to hauling out a rake of carriages for a late summer train from Victoria to Dover on 31 September 1957, Class 'U1' 'Mogul' No 31903 has its coupling checked.

At the present time Stewarts Lane Traction & Rolling Stock Maintenance Depot (as it is now titled) maintains 'Gatwick Express' locomotives and stock for the Intercity Sector, locomotives for Railfreight's Trainload Construction and for the NSE Civil Engineers, and also acts as a stabling point for a variety of South Eastern Section EMUs. Known today as the 'EMU shed', the same premises on 6 April 1992 are occupied by Class '415/4' and '415/7' 4EPBs Nos 5473 and 5627, the latter being one of six EMUs used with 'Kent Coast' express stock and specially geared to run at speeds of up to 90 mph. *R. C. Riley/BM*

South London Line

FACTORY JUNCTION: It was to serve the new suburbs of Brixton, Peckham Rye and Denmark Hill that the LB&SCR opened its South London line between Victoria and London Bridge on 1 August 1865. With a train from Victoria to London Bridge at Wandsworth Road station in the background, Class 'C' 0-6-0 No 31690 negotiates the junction on 27 March 1957 with a small load of milk empties from Morden South to Bollo Lane.

The railway is still in operation today, providing a Monday-to-Saturday half-hour service, although yesterday's suburbs are generally considered as today's inner city. Unfortunately the old signal box window through which Dick Riley took his photograph is now plated up, and another window which provides a slightly different angle had to be used for the present scene. With the roof lights of the building beneath replaced with corrugated iron, the semaphore signals superseded by colour lights, and Wandsworth Road station in the background sporting a new footbridge, Class '73/1' electro-diesel No 73135 passes the same position on 2 May 1990, heading for Stewarts Lane depot with a defective coach that required attention. *R. C. Riley/KB*

CLAPHAM HIGH STREET: On 11 October 1953 a particularly ancient-looking 2NOL EMU, No 1803, restarts from what was then known as Clapham station, with a South London Line train for London Bridge. Introduced in 1934, these two-car units were actually made up from converted LSWR steam stock of much earlier vintage. At this time the station appeared in a reasonable state of repair and sported a platform canopy on the Victoria side as well as its own signal box and attendant semaphores.

By the late 1980s, as seen in the second view, Clapham station was in a particularly run-down condition, with the platform buildings seemingly derelict and held up by scaffolding, and corrugated iron covering the windows on the exit from the dank platform subway. It was no surprise when the station received media attention as the most ill-kept on Network SouthEast!

As indicated by the third view, taken in April 1989, NSE was stung into action by the adverse publicity and the station was soon to be smartened up considerably. By 1991-92 even the South London Line trains themselves were formed mainly of modern Class '456' stock. Now called Clapham High Street station, a particularly marked contrast with the earlier views is provided by new Class '456' EMU No 456024 forming the 09.52 service from Victoria to London Bridge on 4 April 1992. Passing on the ex-LC&DR main line alongside, a Class '415' 4EPB forms the 09.56 train from Victoria to Beckenham Junction. *R. C. Riley/KB/BM*

BRIXTON JUNCTION: Hauling empty coaching stock from Stewarts Lane, Ivatt Class '2MT' 2-6-2T No 41292 passes Brixton Junction on 8 May 1954, heading for Cannon Street.

Half-hourly Victoria-Orpington trains call at Brixton today, but since the closure of East Brixton station in January 1976 it is now bypassed by the South London Line, which crosses above on a recently rebuilt viaduct. Forming a Victoria-Margate service, routed through Catford and Canterbury West, Class '411/5' 4CEP No 1611 passes the same spot on 24 April 1989. Both the Bon Marche and Marks & Spencer buildings are still evident, but Brixton Junction signal box and signal gantry have disappeared. The brick wall on the right has sensibly been surmounted by railings, and the wall on the left has been completely renewed, and provides a walkway to help safeguard the well-being of track maintenance staff. *R. C. Riley/KB*

Surrey Suburbs

COULSDON: Opened in 1899 and originally called Stoats Nest, Coulsdon North station closed on 1 October 1983 with services being diverted to Smitham. With the junction to the station in course of being taken out, but with the signal box still in situ, Class '421/2' 4CIG No 7392 heads a Victoria-Hove-Littlehampton service, via the Quarry Line, on 26 January 1984.

Today no trace remains of the junction or the old box as the 15.30 Victoria-Gatwick Airport 'Gatwick Express' passes, powered by Class '73/2' No 73208 *Croydon 1883-1983*. Travelling in the opposite direction towards Victoria is an 8CIG formation with Class '421/2' No 1258 bringing up the rear. *BM/KB*

SUTTON: The route from West Croydon to Epsom brought Sutton its first trains in 1847, with the Epsom Downs branch following in 1865, and the line from Peckham Rye arriving in 1868. Finally the Southern Railway's line from Wimbledon came into use on 5 January 1930. Formed of a Class '405/2' 4SUB EMU, the 15.52 local service from Horsham to Victoria approaches the Sutton station stop on 5 April 1982.

Still situated at the junction of five lines, today's Sutton commuters enjoy 'South London Lines' trains from London Bridge via Mitcham Junction or West Croydon, services from Victoria to Epsom Downs or Horsham, and can also travel to Guildford or Luton on 'Thameslink'. With both 1982's motive power and signalling already history, the 12.20 Guildford-Luton 'Thameslink' service approaches, as the 12.16 London Bridge-Epsom train departs. The EMUs involved are, respectively, Class '319/0' No 319052 and Class '415/4' 4EPB No 5418. *Both BM*

EPSOM DOWNS (I): The LB&SCR branch to Epsom Downs was opened from Sutton to a terminus about three-quarters of a mile from Epsom Racecourse in May 1865; the branch was electrified in 1928. On 25 March 1980 the 15.38 train from Victoria to Epsom Downs, formed of Class '405/1' 4SUB EMUs Nos 4681 and 4721, passes the terminus signal box as it arrives at the end of its journey.

In 1989 the station was moved some 300 yards north of its former position and a completely new terminus was constructed as part of a new housing estate, the style of the station building being entirely sympathetic to the surrounding houses. The previous four platforms were reduced to one, which accommodates a half-hourly service from Victoria. Taken from the same position on 23 June 1990, the photograph shows a Class '455/8' unit No 5802 awaiting departure as the 09.43 to Victoria. *Both BM*

EPSOM DOWNS (2): The same train seen in the 1980 photograph opposite stands in platform 1 of the old station with the grass-overgrown outer platforms out of use but still visible to left and right, a relic of once-hectic Epsom race days.

A road through the housing estate to the new station now stands where the island platform used to be, demolition of the 1865 LB&SCR station having taken place rapidly on 15-16 February 1989. *Both BM*

TATTENHAM CORNER: Constructed by the SE&CR into the heartlands of the LB&SCR, the branch line from Tadworth to the Tattenham Corner of Epsom Downs racecourse was opened on Derby Day 1901 in open and unashamed competition with its rival. Built right beside the racecourse, the six-platform terminus had more convenient and spacious facilities than Epsom Downs station, and when race traffic was at its peak in the 1920s and 1930s some 60 specials ran to Tattenham Corner on Derby Day, including the Royal Train. After this the need for race specials dwindled as a result of lower race attendances, coupled with increased car ownership. Other than on race days, the present train service outside the rush hours is hourly from Victoria. On 25 March 1980 Class '415/1' 4EPB No 5002 and Class '416/1' 2EPB No 5652 stand at the buffer-stops awaiting their duties.

Currently the station has been smartened up by NSE, and has had modern platform lighting installed. Otherwise the terminus looks very much the same, as Class '455/8' No 5829 awaits departure as the 11.15 service to Victoria, via Purley and East Croydon, a journey scheduled to take 54 minutes. *Both BM*

Euston

EUSTON (I): The London & Birmingham was the first trunk railway in the world. Other lines came into being prior to its 1837 opening, but the London & Birmingham Railway was considered as the greatest railway event of its kind. From early beginnings its London terminus of Euston developed into a rather sprawling and untidy 15-platform station, which was set back off the Euston Road behind the Euston Hotel and the rather grand Doric arch gateway that led to Hardwick's Great Hall of 1849. The original terminus at the foot of Camden bank was gradually swallowed up by the expanding needs of the LNWR until just the hotel, Doric arch and Great Hall survived. At the buffer-stops of platforms 1 and 2 of the old Euston, 'Jubilee' Class 4-6-0 No 45637 *Windward Islands* and original 'Royal Scot' 4-6-0 No 46134 *The Cheshire Regiment* stand with morning arrivals on 1 June 1951.

The remaining landmarks of the old Euston were completely swept away during the construction of the present-day Euston station, opened in October 1968. At platform 2 on 1 April 1992 the 10.30 Intercity service from Manchester Piccadilly has just arrived, headed by non-powered Driving Van Trailer (DVT) No 82131. The locomotive which has provided power for the journey is on the other end of the train. *Both BM*

EUSTON (2): Rebuilt 'Royal Scot' 4-6-0 No 46164 *The Artists' Rifleman* arrives at Euston on 21 August 1951 with the 'Manxman' express from Liverpool Lime Street, so called as it connected with the Isle of Man ferry.

The Euston of today is certainly modern, but to that doubtful epithet must be added the words cold and inhospitable. At the time of the rebuilding considerable pressure was brought to bear upon British Rail to prevent the wholesale destruction of every vestige of the old Euston, including the famous Doric arch, but all to no avail. Under the present-day airport-style structure, the 10.10 Intercity train from Liverpool Lime Street stands in the same position on 1 April 1992, having been brought in by Class '86/1' No 86101 *Sir William A. Stanier FRS* which, instead of propelling the train from the rear, has had to tow its DVT No 82121 as result of a faulty connection with the control wiring through the train. *Both BM*

EUSTON (3): At the 'country end' of Euston station on 3 August 1958 Stanier Class '8F' 2-8-0 No 48122 prepares to haul the ECS of the 'Mancunian' express away to Stonebridge Park carriage depot for servicing, a depot construct-ed in 1953 to supersede the old Willesden Junction carriage sheds. To the rear, departing from platform 4, is one of the LNWR 'Oerlikon' EMUs dating from 1915 and forming a stopping train for Watford Junction.

Departing from the same platform at the Euston of today, Class '86/2' No 86222 *Lloyd's List 250th Anniversary* removes ECS of the 09.29 service from Carlisle, which it is taking to the carriage depot at Stonebridge Park, now given the rather grand title of Wembley Intercity Depot. *Both BM*

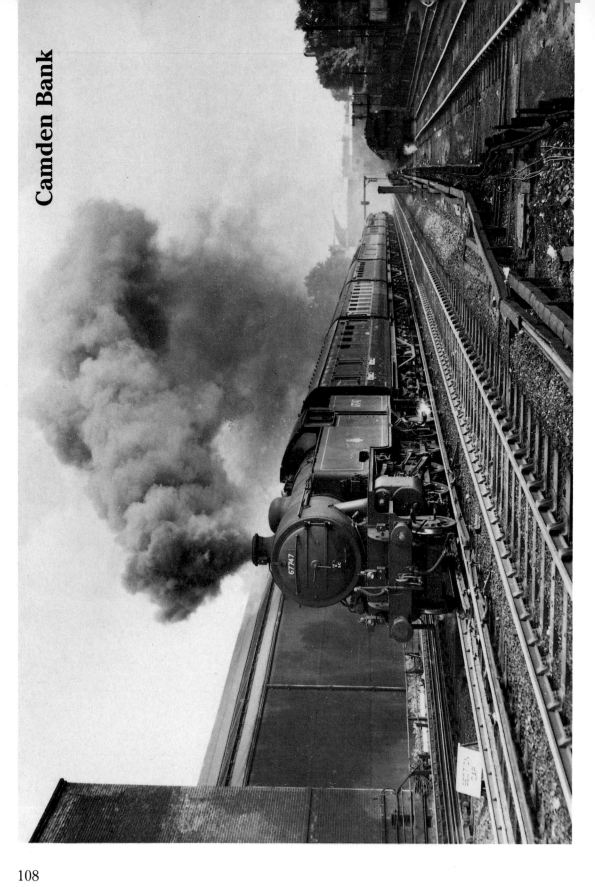

CAMDEN BANK (I): Trains depart from Euston on a down gradient of 1 in 149, levelling to 1 in 575 before coming to the foot of Camden Bank, where a testing assault of 1 in 70 prevails for nearly a mile to the summit at 1 in 77. In steam days locomotives climbing the hill with the heavier expresses often made an impressive sight with wheelslip causing spectacular exhausts. Approaching Camden summit, an unusual sight on 21 September 1958 was Thompson Class 'L1' 2-6-4T No 67747 hauling ECS for Stonebridge Park carriage sheds. The Eastern Region locomotive was allocated to Neasden shed (see page 80), which as 34E came under the auspices of King's Cross (34A). However, Neasden was transferred to the London Midland Region in 1958, and became 14D under Cricklewood. Most of the Eastern Region locomotives were soon to be transferred away, but this one remained long enough to receive a 14D smokebox shedplate, and thus found itself working a duty of this type out of Euston.

Passing the same spot in 1990 Class '321/4' EMU No 321426 forms a semi-fast service from Euston to Milton Keynes. The background has changed out of all recognition, and the underbridge has been opened up, with safety railings installed. The siding on the right has disappeared, but the 'section gap' notice remains in situ on the left. *R. C. Riley/KB*

CAMDEN BANK (2): With a warm autumn sun dissipating the best of the exhaust effect from the chimney, Riddles Standard Class '7MT' 'Pacific' No 70033 *Charles Dickens* hammers up the Bank on 7 October 1958 hauling all-maroon stock forming an express for Manchester (London Road).

Camden bank offers few problems to the electric locomotive-hauled expresses of today, although it is not unknown even for these to suffer wheelslip when rails become wet and greasy. On a very dull but dry morning Class 86/2 No 86233 *Laurence Olivier* climbs the bank without fuss, hauling the 08.20 Intercity service from Euston to Blackpool North. Apart from the obvious accoutrements of the overhead electrification and a much enlarged tree, Camden Bank remains little changed over the years. *Both BM*

Camden (1B)

CAMDEN SHED (I): Major engineering features of the newly-opened London & Birmingham Railway included the great 'Engine House' containing the Camden Bank winding engines and the nearby engine shed. By 1844 locomotives were found to be capable of climbing the Bank unaided and the stationary engines were dispensed with. Locomotive servicing facilities remained, however, with two new sheds being constructed in 1847, one for goods engines on the original site on the east side of the line, and the other for passenger locomotives on the west side. This latter shed was greatly altered and modernised by the LMS and is shown here, as Camden (lB), being passed by 'Patriot' Class '6P' 4-6-0 No 45516 *The Bedfordshire and Hertfordshire Regiment* hauling the 16.47 train from Euston to Northampton and Stafford. The two personages taking photographs on the shed during an official visit by the Railway Photographic Society on 16 July 1958 are Geoff Rixon and, with inevitable tripod, Maurice Earley.

After a spell as a diesel depot from 1962, Camden 'top link' closed in 1966, and the site is now completely taken over by carriage sidings where, on 22 April 1992, a Class '321/4' EMU is being passed by the 15.30 Euston-Crewe Parcels train hauled by 'Rail Express Services' (RES) Class '86/4' No 86401, a locomotive once painted in NSE colours and named *Northampton Town*. *Both BM*

CAMDEN SHED (2): Camden Shed's 70-foot vacuum-operated turntable was installed by the LMS in 1936, replacing a 60-foot turntable which in turn had replaced a 35-foot one installed in 1870. On 16 July 1958 'Patriot' 4-6-0 No 45546 *Fleetwood* is turned ready to back down for 'coaling up' at the coaling plant behind.

The site from the same viewpoint in April 1992 shows a line-up of Class '321/4' EMUs awaiting the evening rush hour, headed by No 321427. The background buildings on the right remain, although their previously blank walls have had windows built in. *Both BM*

CAMDEN SHED (3): In pristine red livery, 'Princess Royal' Class '8P' 'Pacific' No 46200 *The Princess Royal* is turned on the Camden turntable on the same day, in readiness to back down to Euston and take out one of the crack West Coast Main Line expresses of the day.

In 1992 a Class '321/4' rests at the extremity of the present-day Camden sidings in the position where the turntable used to be situated. The buildings at the rear are obviously the same ones which were in the background 34 years before, although they do show a number of alterations which have occurred during the passage of time. *Both BM*

CAMDEN ROUNDHOUSE: Constructed in 1847 on the site of the original London & Birmingham Railway engine shed of 1837, the now-famous 'Roundhouse' in Chalk Farm Road, London NW3, was brick-built to a diameter of 160 feet, and had 24 roads radiating out from a 35-foot centre turntable. As was noted earlier, it was built as a maintenance shed for freight locomotives, with the site on the opposite side of the line being constructed at the same time for passenger types, and surviving to become Camden (lB). The 'Roundhouse', however, was last utilised for railway purposes in 1871, and was leased by the railway to W. & A. Gilbey who used it to store their well-known brand of gin until the listed structure was handed over to the arts in 1964, after which it was used as a theatre. Presently the old building is boarded up, and awaiting a decision as to its future use. Passing the 145-year-old structure on 3 October 1959 with a container freight that could be considered as a forerunner to today's 'Freightliner' workings, Stanier 'Black Five' mixed traffic 4-6-0 No 45111 awaits a clear signal to proceed through Primrose Hill station on the North London Line route to continue its journey northward.

Seen from the same viewpoint on 22 April 1992 Class '90/1' No 90134 passes in the opposite direction with a 'Freightliner' bound for Felixstowe. *R. C. Riley/BM*

CAMDEN SUMMIT: Southwards from Tring, the West Coast route is relatively flat until Camden Bank is reached a mile out of Euston, when trains go 'over the top' to descend into the terminus. Drifting easily down the first part of the bank at 1 in 77, rebuilt 'Patriot' 4-6-0 No 45545 *Planet* **heads an express from Wolverhampton on 3 August 1958.**

On 22 April 1992 RES-liveried Class '90/0' No 90020 *Colonel Bill Cockburn CBE TD* **passes the same location heading for Euston with the 06.30 Parcels service from Glasgow Polmadie.** *Both BM*

PRIMROSE HILL TUNNEL: Just over 1¼ miles from its Euston destination, the 'Emerald Isle Express' from Holyhead bursts from the depths of Primrose Hill tunnel on 6 June 1973, powered by Class '86' No E3106 (now No 86214 *Sans Pareil*).

Mk III DVT No 82152 emerges from the tunnel at the same position on 22 April 1992 heading the 12.55 Wolverhampton-Euston Intercity service, which has Class '86/2' No 86225 *Hardwicke* out of sight in the tunnel providing the necessary traction. A new-style speed restriction sign is in place, and the building above the tunnel has been truncated. The tunnel brickwork itself has been nicely cleaned up. *Both BM*

Willesden (1A)

WILLESDEN SHED: To attend to the needs of their freight locomotives, many railway companies with a London terminus found it necessary to construct an engine shed on the nearest available land outside the capital. To ease pressure on Camden shed, Willesden depot was constructed by the LNWR in 1873 for this purpose and, coded 1A in 1935, was always primarily a freight depot. A view of the shed taken from across the Grand Union Canal *circa* 1936 shows early 'Black Fives', Class '4F' 0-6-0s and 'Jinties' all simmering outside the original 12-road straight shed, a structure substantially unchanged since it was built, although extended in 1898 to enlarge its capacity; the two types of architecture are clearly apparent, and give the building a somewhat hybrid appearance. Willesden-allocated steam engines continued to soldier on powering freights and the like during the advent of dieselisation, but electrification finally rendered the depot redundant; it was closed in September 1965 and afterwards demolished, the site being taken over by the Willesden 'Freightliner' terminal.

From the same position in 1992 it can be seen that a bridge has been constructed across the canal to connect the terminal with the adjacent freight lines, and on the skyline can be seen the variety of prefabricated buildings which have replaced 1A. The present-day Willesden Traction Depot, constructed to maintain the current fleet of electric locomotives, is situated on the other side of the main line. *Lens of Sutton/BM*

Into Middlesex and Herts

WEMBLEY: Apart from the main line itself, the route between Willesden and Wembley Central has always been bordered by extensive sidings and depots throughout its length, variously referred to as Willesden, Stonebridge Park, Brent, Wembley and, latterly, Wembley International Freight Yard. Nearing Wembley Central station on 26 June 1973, the first electric locomotive constructed for the WCML electrification, Class '81' No 81001, heads a Euston-Carlisle District parcels train.

Passing the yards under construction for Channel Tunnel freight traffic at the same place on 11 April 1992, Class '321/4' EMU No 321440 forms the 16.54 semi-fast service from Euston to Birmingham New Street. *Both BM*

SOUTH KENTON: Passing the Middlesex suburbs of South Kenton on 29 August 1964, a fitted freight from Willesden heads northwards in the hands of Stanier 'Black Five' 4-6-0 No 44680.

At the same location just over 15 years later very little appears to have changed apart from the tree growth as Class '85' No 85030 accelerates north with the 12.43 'Silcock & Collins Express' of covered 'cartics'. The train has begun its journey from the Ford Motor Company plant sidings at Dagenham Dock, with Liverpool Garston as its destination. All the first-generation WCML electric locomotives of Classes '81' to '85' have now been withdrawn from service. *P. J. Lynch/BM*

BUSHEY TROUGHS (I): Despite Nationalisation having taken place some three years earlier, the legend 'LMS' still appears on the tender of unrebuilt 'Royal Scot' 4-6-0 No 46110 *Grenadier Guardsman* on 19 May 1951 as the locomotive scoops up a little too much water from Bushey troughs on the way northwards with an express from Euston to Llandudno and Holyhead.

Modern electric traction has no need of water troughs. With those at Bushey having been taken out in the 1960s, the 15.00 Intercity express from Euston to Birmingham New Street passes the site on 11 April 1992 powered by as yet un-named Class '90' No 90003. *Both BM*

121

BUSHEY TROUGHS (2): Seen from the same vantage point as the view on the previous pages, but with the camera pointing in the opposite direction, 'Princess Royal' 'Pacific' No 46207 *Princess Arthur of Connaught* has no need of water replenishment while passing over Bushey troughs on 25 March 1953 with a Euston-bound express from Scotland.

Passing the same four-arch bridge on 11 April 1992, the 13.48 express from Birmingham New Street has 16 miles to travel before coming to rest at the Euston buffer-stops. Leading the train is Mk III DVT No 82138, while providing traction and propelling from the rear is Class '87/0' No 87025 *County of Cheshire*. *Both BM*

BUSHEY: Between Bushey station (or Bushey & Oxhey as it was then called) and the troughs once stood the large water-softening tower which supplied water to the pick-up channels. Passing the building on the same day in 1953 ex-LNWR Class 'G2a' 0-8-0 No 49450 trundles towards London hauling wooden-sided coal wagons.

Scurrying past the same position on 11 April 1992, a Milton Keynes-Euston semi-fast service is in the hands of Class '321/4' EMU No 321431. The water tower has gone together with the centre road siding, modern flat-bottom track has replaced the old bullhead variety, and the embankment has become an almost impenetrable woodland. *Both BM*

WATFORD JUNCTION (I): Hauling the 15 coaches of the 10.40 Euston-Carlisle express, 'Princess Coronation' Class '8P' 'Pacific' No 46229 *Duchess of Hamilton* (now preserved as part of the National Collection and still working on the main line today) hammers past Watford No 1 signal box on a wet 9 August 1952.

On 11 April 1992 the 12.00 Euston-Wolverhampton Intercity express rushes through Watford and passes the same position, unusually powered by a pair of Class '86/2' electric locomotives, No 86210 *City of Edinburgh* and No 86258 *Talyllyn - The First Preserved Railway*. The signal box and semaphore signals have been superseded by Watford power box (out of the picture to the right) and colour light signals, one of the two nearside tracks has been removed, and lineside electrical boxes and overhead catenary masts now clutter the scene. In fact, all that seems to have visibly improved is the weather! *Both BM*

WATFORD JUNCTION (2): Watford is designated as a junction because of the branch line to St Albans Abbey station, a distance of 6¼ miles. In August 1952 the branch service was being operated by ACV demonstration railcars Nos 1, 2 and 3, seen here forming the 17.48 to Abbey station alongside a Class '7F' 'G2a' 0-8-0 No 49145 which is coming off shed in order to take out a freight for Bescot from the adjacent yards.

The bay platform for St Albans Abbey trains, together with the site of Watford shed (1C), is now a car park, and the through line on the other side of the platform is now used for the branch trains which were in the hands of Class '313' EMUS from electrification in July 1988, but are now operated by Class '321s'. On 11 April 1992 unit No 321428 was operating the 'Abbey Flyer' shuttle, and can just be seen over the fence, having discharged its passengers after arrival as the 13.30 from St Albans, returning from Watford as the 13.50. *Both BM*

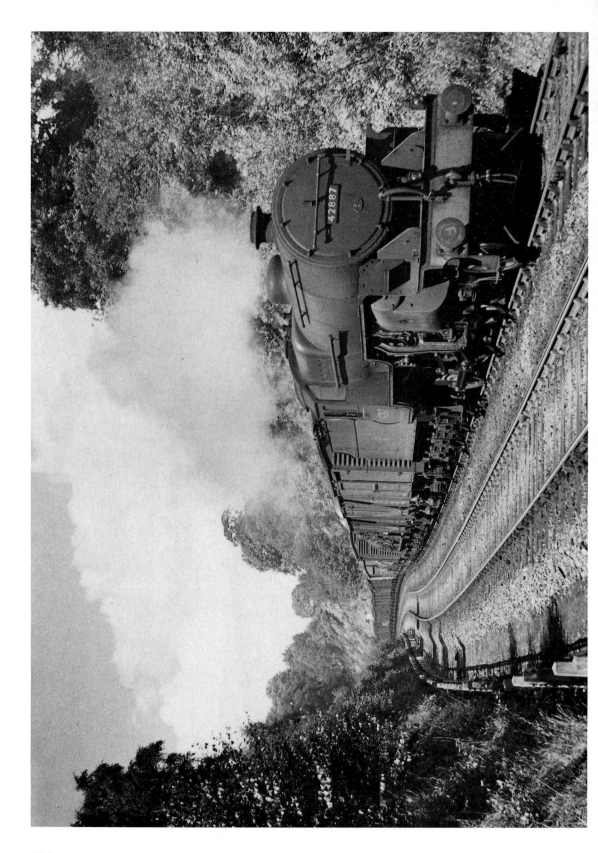

WATFORD CUTTING (I): Manchester Longsight-allocated Class '5MT' 'Crab' 2-6-0 No 42887 snakes around the curves of the WCML slow lines south of Watford tunnel on 9 August 1952, hauling a fitted freight of impressive length bound for Willesden.

At the same location on 11 April 1992 the 09.10 Intercity service from Liverpool Lime Street to Euston is headed by Mk III DVT No 82131, with Class '86/1' No 86101 *Sir William A. Stanier FRS* providing traction, propelling out of sight at the rear. The DVT has its usual sleek front-end appearance slightly marred by one jumper cable cover being in the raised position with the other one correctly closed. Apart from the trappings of electrification, Watford cutting has changed little over the years. *Both BM*

WATFORD CUTTING (2): Bursting from the southern portal of Watford tunnel on 9 August 1952 'Royal Scot' Class '7P' 4-6-0 No 46135 *The East Lancashire Regiment* **approaches Watford on the fast line with the 'Merseyside Express' from Liverpool Lime Street incorporating through coaches from Southport.**

On 11 April 1992 the 09.36 'Little Euston' semi-fast service from Birmingham New Street to Euston is seen at the same place, formed of Class '321/4' EMU No 321440. *Both BM*

St Pancras

ST PANCRAS (1): The Midland Railway opened its London terminus at the eastern end of the Euston Road in 1868 and it took its name from the parish in which it was constructed. For nearly a century the train shed, engineerd by W. H. Barlow, had the largest station roof in the world without internal supports. Giving some indication of dramatic Victorian engineering at its finest, the lofty single span overall roof provides a background to Stanier Class '3MT' 2-6-2T No 40172 on 3 August 1958 as it awaits to depart for Cricklewood sidings with the ECS of an earlier arrival from Leicester.

Although the early colour light signals and platform lighting have been updated, trackwork and platforms have been altered, and the accoutrements of overhead electrification intrude, the HSTs of today still look strangely out of place in the same setting. On 13 April 1992 'Intercity 125' services for Sheffield and Nottingham respectively await departure with Class '43' power cars Nos 43074 and 43083 leading. *Both BM*

ST PANCRAS (2): Nearly as famous as the St Pancras train shed are the adjacent gas holders, some of which, like St Pancras station building, are the subject of a preservation order. On 14 May 1955 'Jubilee' Class '6P' 4-6-0 No 45589 *Gwalior* makes a smokey start from the old Midland terminus with the 16.15 train for Leeds and Bradford.

With an engineer's occupation near Wembley requiring services from Liverpool and Holyhead to use the facilities of St Pancras instead of Euston, Mk III DVT No 82112 departs on 13 October 1991 leading the 11.39 Intercity service to Liverpool Lime Street, powered from the rear by Class '87/0' No 87026 *Sir Richard Arkwright*. A lengthened platform has resulted in changes to the track layout, and the semaphore signalling has gone together with the most distant gas holder. *P. J. Lynch/BM*

130

CAMBRIDGE STREET DEPOT: Just as in the case of Ranelagh Bridge, Paddington (page 13), diesel locomotives arriving at St Pancras were able to avoid fuelling trips to Cricklewood by using the fuelling depot at Cambridge Street, a short way out from the terminus. Ranelagh Bridge was made redundant when the HSTs were introduced, and a few years later the same fate befell Cambridge Street. On 9 March 1978 Class '47/4' No 47491 and Class '45/1' 'Peak' No 45123 *The Lancashire Fusilier* attend for fuelling.

In April 1992 only the old buffer-stop remains as evidence that the depot ever existed. *Both BM*

Kentish Town (14B)

KENTISH TOWN SHED (I): Kentish Town was the Midland Railway's London passenger depot, and opened along with the company's London extension to St Pancras in 1867-68. A number of alterations and enlargements were made at various times over the years and the shed was a busy one, as it not only had its own allocation of over 100 locomotives, but was also responsible for servicing the motive power arriving at St Pancras from other major depots such as Derby, Leicester, Nottingham and Sheffield. Dieselisation on the Midland main line, and in particular the advent of the Rolls Royce-engined Class '127' DMUs on local services, rendered the depot facilities redundant quite early, and closure came about in 1963. Standing inside 'No l' shed, or the 'Metro' as it was better known, 1878 Johnson-designed ex-Midland Class '1F' 0-6-0T No 41724, used for shunting and local goods workings, poses for the camera on 19 December 1954. Following Second World War bomb damage, the roof here was eventually replaced in 1958.

The old 14B complex today is occupied by J. Murphy & Sons (Contractors) Ltd, to whom thanks are due for enabling the present-day comparision views to be taken. Both BM

KENTISH TOWN SHED (2): Until Cricklewood shed (14A) opened in 1882, Kentish Town was known simply as 'London'. On 15 June 1955 1911-designed Fowler Class '4F' 0-6-0 No 43964 stands outside the depot minus a connecting rod.

With the background chimney providing a reference point, the present-day view looks across the contractor's yard. *Both BM*

CRICKLEWOOD SHED: Following the opening of the Midland's London extension, sidings for freight sorting were laid outside the capital at Brent, and a small four-road shed, 'Hendon', was opened in 1870. This became inadequate for the company's burgeoning freight traffic, and a new roundhouse was constructed in 1882, known until the turn of the century as Childs Hill. In 1893 a second roundhouse was added, followed by a fitting shop and a number of other enlargements. Now known as Cricklewood, the depot had an allocation in the 1950s of over 80 engines, although these numbers had reduced considerably by the time a few of those from Kentish Town arrived after that shed closed. On 28 November 1954 one of seven Stanier 'Black Fives' fitted with Caprotti valve gear and Timken roller bearings, No 44754, stands outside the depot awaiting a return working home to Leeds Holbeck (20A).

Later a new diesel depot opened on the opposite side of the line, being known as Cricklewood East and assuming the mantle of 14A, the original complex becoming 14B Cricklewood West. Decreasing numbers of locomotives used the original facility, until steam was finally banished from the Midland line on 14 December 1964. Diesel traction used the premises as a stabling point for a time thereafter, but the buildings were eventually demolished and, as shown below, the site has now been taken over by a large Royal Mail 'Parcel Force' depot. *Both BM*

CRICKLEWOOD DIESEL DEPOT: Following the demise of Cricklewood West, the diesel depot became plain Cricklewood, and was responsible for maintaining both main-line and freight locomotives in addition to the DMU commuter fleet. On 29 October 1978 Class '45/0' 'Peaks' Nos 45065, 45077 and 45042 await their next duties alongside Class '25/2' No 25117.

Despite being relatively modern, this depot itself closed in 1987 following the electrification of the local services to Bedford and the main-line workings being taken over by HSTs. A building to stable EMUs was constructed a short distance down the line, but this had no official motive power allocation; it has now been taken over by Charterail Ltd. On 21 April 1992 the depot buildings still stand but are no longer in use. *Both BM*

The Midland Main Line

BRENT YARDS: With a long haul of coal wagons from the Midlands, BR Standard Class '9F' 2-10-0 No 92009 arrives at Brent Yards, Cricklewood, passing between Brent Junction No 1 and No 2 signal boxes on 19 March 1955. Two steel-sided wagons are next to the locomotive, but the rest of the rolling-stock still consists of much older wooden-bodied vehicles.

Although rationalised and reduced in area, the yards at Brent are still important for today's transfer freight. Passing the same location on 4 May 1990, Class '319/0' 'Thameslink' units Nos 319032 and 319019 glide past heading away from the camera, forming the 18.52 service from St Pancras to Bedford. *R. C. Riley/BM*

HENDON: Passing Hendon on the same day in 1955, another Riddles-designed BR Standard '9F' 2-10-0 heads for Brent Yards with a similar haul of coal from Toton Yards. This train has a few more steel wagons interspersed among the wooden ones than the example opposite, and the locomotive itself, No 92045, is a later one with a more modern Type BR1C tender.

Embankment foliage prevents an exactly similar angle being obtained for a present-day view. However, at the same location on 16 May 1990 a test train from Derby Research & Technical Centre heads southwards, hauled by one of the Research Centre's own allocated Class '47/4' locomotives, No 47973 (since named *Derby Evening Telegraph*). The location is much the same as in the past, although the bridge spanning Hendon station has been modified to allow for the installation of the overhead electrification catenary. *R. C. Riley/KB*

SILKSTREAM JUNCTION: Situated just north of Hendon, Silkstream Junction originally marked the bifurcation of the southbound slow lines into Local and Goods lines, the latter passing over the down Local and up and down Fast lines by a flyover to form six running lines between here and Finchley Road. With the junction signal box in the distance, a St Albans-St Pancras stopping train takes the up Local and heads for the Hendon stop on 25 May 1957, hauled by Fairburn Class '4MT' 2-6-4T No 42178.

Forming the 11.37 Bedford-Brighton 'Thameslink' service on 18 September 1988, Class '319' No 319055 passes the once rural-looking scene. Behind the fencing today is the M1 motorway! *Both BM*

MILL HILL BROADWAY: Pulling away from the Mill Hill Broadway stop on 25 May 1957, Fairburn Class '4MT' 2-6-4T No 42680 hauls the 16.40 local train from St Pancras to St Albans.

With the northbound carriageway of the M1 motorway now running through where the background houses used to be, Class '319/0' 'Thameslink' EMU No 319057 restarts the 11.20 Guildford-Luton train away from the station, as the rear of a train of empty spoil wagons from Forders Sidings, Stewartby, to Chatham Dockyard can be seen proceeding in the opposite direction. *Both BM*

ELSTREE & BOREHAMWOOD (I): Although the Beyer-Garratt type of locomotive was very successful in Africa, it found little demand in its British homeland. The LNER had one, but the only others in main-line use within these shores were the 33 2-6-6-2Ts which worked Toton-Brent coal trains for some 30 years. Approaching Elstree tunnel on the up slow line from the north on 12 April 1952, No 47994 heads a typical coal train of the day and passes under the boxed-in sewage outlet pipe that once crossed the tracks here.

With the pipe now removed to make way for the overhead electrification catenary, Class '56' No 56057 passes the same spot on 13 April 1992, hauling a Shanks & McEwan train of empty household waste containers, returning to their Cricklewood Depot from the landfill site at Forders Sidings, near Stewartby, in Bedfordshire. *Both BM*

ELSTREE & BOREHAMWOOD (2): On the same day in 1952 'Jubilee' Class 4-6-0 No 45568 *Western Australia* hammers through the down fast line cutting away from Elstree tunnel hauling the 'Thames-Clyde Express' from St Pancras to Glasgow St Enoch.

Embankment foliage looks to be getting out of hand as the 11.30 St Pancras-Nottingham HST charges past on 13 April 1992, headed by Class '43' power car No 43056 with its *University of Bradford* nameplates missing. *Both BM*

ELSTREE TUNNEL: Taking trains beneath the South Herts plateau, the twin-bore Elstree tunnel was a major engineering accomplishment required for the Midland Railway to achieve its 'London Extension' of 1868. On 25 May 1957 BR Standard Class '9F' 2-10-0 No 92058 emerges from the fast line tunnel with a Toton-bound coal train from Brent.

At the same location on 13 April 1992 Class '319/1' 'Thameslink' EMU No 319171 emerges from the 1,058-yard bore forming the 09.30 Brighton-Bedford train. *Both BM*

INDEX OF LOCATIONS

Acton Wells Junction 75

Barnes 67
Berrylands 60
Brent Yards 136
Brentford Dock 24
Brixton Junction 98
Bushey & Oxhey 123
Bushey troughs 120-122

Cambridge Street Depot (St
  Pancras) 131
Camden Bank 108-110
  summit 115
Camden shed 111-114
  roundhouse 114
Chelsea & Fulham 29
Chelsea Bridge (Cremorne
  Viaduct) 30-31
Chessington South 63
Clapham cutting 52
Clapham High Street 97
Clapham Junction 49-51
Coulsdon North 99
Cremorne Viaduct (Chelsea
  Bridge) 30-31
Cricklewood sheds 134-135

Dalston (Western Junction) 4
Denham 84-85
Durnsford Road
  (Wimbledon) 53

Elstree & Borehamwood 140-
  141
Elstree tunnel 142-143
Epsom 64
Epsom Downs 102-103
Euston 105-107
  Camden Bank 108-110

Factory Junction
  (Wandsworth Road) 96
Feltham shed 69-70

Gerrards Cross 86-87
Gospel Oak 72

Hampstead Heath 73
Hampton Court branch 62
Harrow-on-the-Hill 89
Hendon 137
Hounslow Junction 68

Iver 27

Kensal Green Junction 74
Kensington Olympia
  (Addison Road) 32-33
Kentish Town shed 132-133
Kingston 65

Marylebone 76-79
Merton Abbey 58
Mill Hill Broadway 139

Neasden shed 80
Nine Elms 45-48
  Loco Junction 45
North Acton 6
North Pole Junction 34-35
Northolt Junction 81-82
Northwick Park 88
Northwood Hills 90

Old Oak Common 15-18

Paddington 9-11
  Ranelagh Bridge 12
  Ranelagh Bridge Depot 13
Primrose Hill tunnel 116
Putney 66

Raynes Park 59

St Pancras 129-131
Silkstream Junction
  (Hendon) 138
Slough 28
South Kenton 119
South Ruislip 83
Southall 20-22
  shed 23
Staines West 26
Stewarts Lane chord 46-47
Stewarts Lane shed 94-95
Surbiton 61
Sutton 100-101

Tattenham Corner 104

Upper Holloway 71
Uxbridge Vine Street 25

Vauxhall 44
Victoria 91-93

Wandsworth Road (Factory
  Junction) 96
Waterloo 36-43
Waterloo & City Railway 40-
  41
Watford Junction 124-125
Watford tunnel 126-128
Wembley 118
West Ealing 19
West London Sidings (Old
  Oak Common) 14
Willesden shed 117
Wimbledon 55-57
  Durnsford Road 53
Wimbledon Park Carriage
  Sidings 54